VOCABULARY CONNECTIONS

Book III
Academic Vocabulary

VOCABULARY
CONNECTIONS

Book III
Academic Vocabulary

Marianne C. Reynolds
Mercer County Community College

Boston   Burr Ridge, IL   Dubuque, IA   Madison, WI
New York   San Francisco   St. Louis
Bangkpk   Bogotá   Caracas   Lisbon   London   Madrid   Mexico City
Milan   New Delhi   Seoul   Singapore   Sydney   Taipei   Toronto

McGraw-Hill College

A Division of The **McGraw·Hill** *Companies*

VOCABULARY CONNECTIONS: BOOK III ACADEMIC VOCABULARY

This book is printed on acid-free paper.

5 6 7 8 9 10   QPF/QPF   0 5 4 3 2

ISBN 0-07-052626-5

Editorial director: *Phillip A. Butcher*
Sponsoring editor: *Sarah Moyers*
Editor assistant: *Rebecca Andersons*
Marketing manager: *Lesley Denton*
Project manager: *Christine Parker*
Production supervisor: *Lori Koetters*
Freelance design coordinator: *Laurie J. Entringer*
Cover design: *Z-Graphics*
Supplement coordinator: *Jennifer L. Frazier*
Compositor: *Electronic Publishing Services, Inc.*
Typeface: *10/12 Palatino*
Printer: *Quebecor Printing Book Group/Fairfield*

http://www.mhhe.com

For Shahid, Katie, Ozzie,
Cathy, Kana, and all my other
students who helped me develop
and try out the exercises in this book

PREFACE

Many people would like to have a larger vocabulary. If you check the "self-help" section of a bookstore, you may find several books devoted to helping people learn more words. As with many other subjects, though, vocabulary is hard to learn on your own. Most of us benefit from the discipline and schedule a course provides that independent study does not. In addition to the advantage of studying vocabulary in a college course, you also have the benefit of additional exposure to a variety of words in your other courses and academic activities. The business you are in as a college student is "word dependent." In your classes and your studies, you are constantly bombarded with words. You hear them; you see them; you write them. If you make a conscious effort to learn and remember the meanings of new words, you will find your "environment of words" a great help.

We can expand our vocabulary in several ways. As children, part of our normal development is language acquisition. For young children learning to speak, the rate of new vocabulary words learned is phenomenal. They usually begin to use new words as labels for people close to them (Mommy) or familiar objects (cookie). Adults who learn a new language also may begin by asking the names of objects: "What is this called?" or "How do you say *casa* (house) in English?" For both groups, this language learning is an exciting and rewarding process. Those of you who begin to work or study in a new field will also be exposed to a new vocabulary. A student who began a new job in a warehouse learned the term "palletizing." Computer science students may learn a new meaning for the word "bursting," as it applies to paper instead of balloons.

As college students, your vocabulary development may not be as dramatic as that of a young child or a non-native speaker's experience. You will learn new words as you read and listen. Your professors may use words with which you are unfamiliar, and you may meet new words in your textbooks and course-related reading. In many cases, these words will be the same, and the more often you meet them, the more likely you are to learn and remember their meanings. A conscious effort on your part will make learning vocabulary easier, too. You may even enjoy it!

You must learn to look for clues as you hear or read an unfamiliar word. In class, your professor may spontaneously provide a definition, or a student may ask for one. You may be able to tell the word's meaning from the context, the way it is used. The speaker's gestures or tone of voice, or the spelling of the word on the board, may help as well. In print, too, you can use the context, a supplied definition, a glossary, and your dictionary as aids.

If you had the luxury of unlimited time to expand your vocabulary, you could probably rely solely on your exposure to new words, terms, and phrases. To be a successful college learner, though, you should probably make a more deliberate effort to learn most of the words you will meet in college situations. The English language is rich with synonyms that allow readers and speakers to select words that clearly and specifically communicate their meanings. As a reader and listener, you will learn the meanings of many words that can be used interchangeably. Although it is admirable if you choose to incorporate many of the words you learn this semester into your speaking and writing vocabulary, your primary goal this semester should be recognition. When you complete the work in this textbook, you still may not be able to write from memory all the definitions you learned. If you learned them well, however, when you first studied them, you should be able to recall their meanings when you meet them in context in the future.

The texts in this series are designed to be practical. The three books can be used in any order. In fact, the order of the chapters within each book can be changed as well.

The first book deals with general vocabulary. Many college professors claim that they can teach their students the course-related terminology, but they also expect them to be knowledgeable about general, frequently used, college-level words. In this book, you will learn many words that can neither be defined by their word parts nor associated with a particular field. They are words that will come up in lectures, textbooks, newspaper and journal articles, and conversation among educated people. They were selected from high-frequency word lists, so you know you can count on seeing them again. Many instructors choose to begin with this book and teach the word parts and academic words later in the semester.

The second book concentrates on word parts—prefixes, suffixes, and roots. You will learn the meanings of the word parts and many words they make up. You may begin to think of words as puzzles. You can analyze words by identifying their parts to discover their meanings. You can also synthesize the word parts by putting them together to make new words. Learning word parts is a very efficient way to increase your vocabulary. There are many English words that can be defined if you know the meanings of their parts. The benefits of your study time will be multiplied as you are able to unlock the meanings of a tremendous number of words. You will also find yourself using word parts of words you already know to help define new ones.

The third book represents words in academic context. College students take reading or first-year experience courses to help them do well in their college course work. The most practical way to teach you how to define unfamiliar words when you meet them in your textbooks is to give you some samples. The subject fields are representative of courses most college students take during their first or second year. Certainly you won't learn all the vocabulary you need for your psychology or biology course in one chapter. You will, though, learn some key terms in each field and practice using textbook material to define them. You may also be surprised at how many of these terms are defined in the text and how many others' meanings you can figure out.

In addition to working through the exercises in this book and studying for the quizzes and tests, you may want to keep a personal journal. Some students find it beneficial to keep a record of unfamiliar words they meet on a daily basis. A note indicating the word, where you encountered it, and a brief definition is all that is necessary. Many of my students report that they find themselves recording the same word several times until they learn it. This experience seems to show the need to study as well as write down unfamiliar words. It also supports the notion that some words occur more frequently than others and recommends their mastery. Research has shown that recreational or "free reading" also increases vocabulary development. Many college students complain that they barely have time to complete their course-related reading. Those who can, though, devote twenty minutes a day to reading for pleasure (a newspaper, magazine, novel, or nonfiction book) report a gain in word knowledge as well as other benefits.

Study often. Brief daily study sessions are better than a long cramming session just before a test. Study with classmates, discuss the meanings of the words, and make them your own. Tell someone who is curious about words an interesting new term you have learned. Ask someone to quiz you on the word meanings. Try to use one new word a day in your conversation or writing. Pay attention to words and don't be afraid to try them out. You may be surprised at the people who are interested in the origins of words and their meanings.

Marianne C. Reynolds

CONTENTS

Book III

INTRODUCTION:
ACADEMIC CONTEXT

After you complete your reading course, you probably don't expect to take a "vocabulary test" again. You may be surprised to learn, however, that many college professors give "vocabulary tests"; they just have other names for them. For example, your computer science professor may announce a quiz on the *terminology* in the first chapter. Your nursing professor might ask you to write a report on a patient's digestive system, using the correct *medical language*. A history professor could require an essay on contemporary politics and ask you to *define the terms* **liberal** and **conservative.** Vocabulary study and expectation of word knowledge do not end when your reading course requirement is satisfied.

In this book, you will meet academic terms in the context of their field of study. You will practice defining psychology, biology, history, math, and communication terms as you would meet them in a textbook chapter. As you learn the words or phrases, you will also learn a bit more about the field itself. One chapter per field is really just a taste of what the content and terminology of each subject is like. As you study each field in more depth in future courses, you will be expanding your background knowledge and adding to your own context about the field. As with comprehension, you will observe that the more interest and knowledge you have for a particular subject, the easier it is to figure out and learn its terminology. For the fields in which you are not particularly interested, you may have to work harder. In some cases, motivation and curiosity can make up for lack of interest or background knowledge.

As in the other books in this series, there are exercises for practice as well as quizzes that will allow you to demonstrate your knowledge. All the activities and studying can be done independently. However, if you work with others, you will probably find the tasks easier and more enjoyable. You will probably learn more as well. Learning the academic vocabulary in this section of the text collaboratively will give you a taste of group study sessions that many content-area professors recommend. Your instructor may provide class time for you to work with others on some of these exercises, or you may set up your own study or homework groups.

You will find challenging material in this text that will give you a sense of the expectations of college-level courses. Take this opportunity, with the help of your instructor and fellow students, to learn the material—content as well as vocabulary, as you would if you were a student in a psychology, communication, or music class. The exercises ask that you learn the content and apply it, just as you will be expected to do when you take these courses. And you will be a bit more knowledgeable about the field than some of your future fellow students may be.

PRONUNCIATION KEY

Use the following simple pronunciation guide to help you pronounce the words you will study. A sample word is provided for each vowel symbol that is used in the word lists.

	Short Vowels (indicated with no mark)		*Long Vowels* (indicated with a straight line called a macron above the letter)
a	hat	ā	say, hate
e	bet	ē	me, seat
i	tin	ī	fine, sky
o	pot	ō	so, rode
u	cut	ū	mule, use

The schwa (ə) is a very common sound in the English language. It has the sound of "uh" and can be made by any vowel. Examples follow:

a	in above	(ə buv′)
e	in system	(sis′ təm)
u	in circus	(sûr′ kəs)

The doubled oo takes on a short or long sound, too.

Short		*Long*	
oo	cook	o̅o̅	boot

Additional Vowel Sounds

ä	father	ô	order, raw
â	air	û	term, urge

COMMUNICATION: TYPES OF NONVERBAL COMMUNICATION

1

In this chapter, you will read about types of nonverbal communication and learn some vocabulary words that will help your understanding. First you will read an excerpt from a communications textbook. Some of the terms in the reading will be numbered and underlined. Your first task will be to define them either from context or from the stated definition. In the exercises that follow, you will practice using the terms.

Communication is a field that seems to develop and expand almost on a daily basis. We read about the communications revolution and marvel at how quickly information can be accessed or transmitted. Colleges offer a variety of courses that are labeled as communication. You may take a course in radio or television production in the telecommunications department. Some English departments offer communications courses. A communications course may focus on teaching students to speak to groups. A psychology department may offer a course that teaches how to analyze verbal and nonverbal communication. One point of agreement seems to be that communication is a necessary ingredient in a college education, and is essential for living in today's world.

Read the following selection about types of nonverbal communication to learn something about how we send messages without using speech.

TYPES OF NONVERBAL COMMUNICATION

Paralanguage

(1) <u>**Paralanguage**</u> is the way we say something. For example, a father calls his son from another room. From the tone of his father's voice, the child can gauge whether the call is urgent enough to come right away or whether he can watch another minute or so of television. The tone of voice in this example is paralanguage.

A clear distinction exists between a person's use of words (verbal communication) and a person's use of paralanguage (nonverbal communication). Paralanguage includes such vocal characteristics as rate (speed of speaking), pitch (highness or lowness of tone), volume (loudness), and quality (pleasing or unpleasant sound). When any or all of these factors are added to words, they can (2) <u>modify</u> meaning. Albert Mehrabian estimates that 39 percent of the meaning in communication is affected by vocal cues—not the words themselves but the way in which they are said. In languages other than English, this percentage may be even higher.

Rate

The **rate** (speed) at which one speaks can have an effect on the way a message is received. Researchers have studied people speaking at rates varying from 120 words per minute (wpm) to 261 wpm. They discovered that when a speaker uses a faster rate, he or she is seen as more (3) <u>competent</u>. Of course, if you speak too quickly, people won't be able to follow you, and your (4) <u>articulation</u> may also suffer.

Pitch

(5) <u>Pitch</u> refers to the highness or lowness of the voice. Pitch can determine whether a voice sounds pleasant or unpleasant. Some people believe that high-pitched voices are not as pleasant as low-pitched ones. However, the same researchers who studied rate of speaking also found that speakers were judged more competent if they used a higher and varied pitch. Lower pitches are more difficult to hear, and people who have low-pitched voices may be (6) <u>perceived</u> as (7) <u>insecure</u> or shy because they don't seem to speak up. Pitch can be changed, but it requires working with someone who has had professional training in voice modification.

Volume

The meaning of a message can also be affected by its **volume**—how loudly we speak. A loud voice is fine if it's appropriate to the speaker's purpose and is not used all the time. The same is true of a soft voice. Expert teachers know at what points to increase or decrease their volume when they want a class to be quiet.

Vocal Fillers

(8) <u>Vocal fillers</u> are the sounds we use to fill out our sentences or to cover up when we are searching for words. Nonwords such as *uh, er,* and *um* and phrases such as *you know* are a nonverbal way of indicating that we are temporarily stuck and are searching for the right word. We all use vocal fillers; they become a problem only when we use them (9) <u>excessively</u> or if they are distracting to listeners.

Quality

The overall (10) **quality** of a voice is made up of all other vocal characteristics—(11) <u>tempo</u>, (12) <u>resonance</u>, (13) <u>rhythm</u>, pitch, and articulation. Voice quality is important because researchers have found that people with attractive voices are seen as more powerful, more competent, and more honest. However, people with immature voices were seen as less competent and powerful but more honest and warm.

Many of us do not have a very good idea of how we sound. Our classroom experience has been that when students see and hear themselves on videotape, they are almost always more unhappy with how they sound than with how they look. Voices can be changed with hard work and professional assistance.

Body Movement

Body movement, also called (14) *kinesics,* is responsible for a lot of our nonverbal communication. P. Ekman and W. V. Friesen, researchers on nonverbal communication, divide body movements into five categories: emblems, illustrators, regulators, displays of feeling, and adaptors.

Emblems

(15) <u>Emblems</u> are body movements that have a direct translation into words. The extended thumb of the hitchhiker is an emblem that means "I want a ride." A circle made with the thumb and index finger can be translated into "OK." These emblems are known by most of the people in our society, and they are used to send a specific message. Emblems often cannot be carried from one culture to another. If you shake your head back and forth in southern India, for example, it means "yes."

Emblems are often used when words are (16) <u>inappropriate</u>. It would be impractical for a hitchhiker to stand on the side of the road and shout, "Please give me a ride!" Sometimes emblems can replace talk. We cover our faces with our hands if we are embarrassed, and we hold up our fingers to show how many we want. Also, subgroups in a society often use emblems that members of the group understand but whose meanings are intentionally kept from outsiders—the secret handshake of a fraternity is an example.

Illustrators

(17) <u>Illustrators</u> accent, emphasize, or reinforce words. If someone asks how big your suitcase is, you will probably describe it with words and illustrate the dimensions with your hands. If someone is giving you directions, she will probably point down the road and gesture left or right at the appropriate points. Illustrators can help to make communication more exact. If someone tells you he caught a huge fish, you will have an idea of how big the fish was by how far apart he holds his hands. He could tell you the size in inches, but you will get an even better idea if he uses his hands as illustrators. But not all illustrators are gestures. When an instructor underlines something she has written on the blackboard, she is telling you that this point is particularly important. When a car salesperson slams the car door, you can hear how solid it sounds and assume the car is well built.

Regulators

(18) <u>Regulators</u> control the back-and-forth flow of speaking and listening. They include the head nods, hand gestures, shifts in posture, and other body movements that signal the beginning and end of interactions. At a very simple level, a teacher uses a regulator when she points to the person she wants to speak next. On a more subtle level, someone might turn away slightly when you are talking—perhaps indicating "I don't like what I'm hearing" or "I don't want to continue this conversation."

Displays of Feelings

(19) <u>Displays of feelings</u> show, through our faces and our body movements, how intensely we are feeling. If you walk into a professor's office and the professor says, "I can see you are really feeling upset," he or she is responding to nonverbal cues you are giving about your feelings. You could also come in with a body posture indicating "I'm really going to argue about this grade"—with your (20) <u>jutting</u> jaw or stiff body position showing that you are ready for a confrontation.

Exercise 1: Summary

Before you begin to zero in on the underlined words in the passage, try to talk with a fellow student about the content of the passage. Then, in your own words, write a brief summary of what you have learned about types of nonverbal communication. Include some specific ways we communicate without using words.

_____

_____

_____

_____

_____

Exercise 2: Example

Give an example of a situation in which you interpreted a person's paralanguage or body motions to find out his or her mood or intention.

_____

_____

_____

_____

_____

Exercise 3: Definitions

Working on your own or with a fellow student, try to define the underlined words from the selection you have just read. In many cases, you can find the definition in the text. The notation "(stated)" will tell you when this is so. For other terms, you will need to rely on the context and your own background knowledge. Write each definition in the space provided after the word.

1. paralanguage (stated)

   the way we say something .

2. modify

   determine /understand

3. competent

   intelligent —

4. articulation

_____

5. pitch (stated)

highness or lowness in your voice

6. perceived

known

7. insecure

unsure or not confident in themselves

8. vocal fillers (stated)

Sounds we used to fill a pause in sent. or to cover up when we are searching for word

9. excessively

too much

10. quality

(greatness) how good something is.

11. tempo

_____

12. resonance

_____

13. rhythm

beat

14. kinesics (stated)

body movement

15. emblems (stated)

body movements that have a direct translation into words.

16. inappropriate

not proper

17. illustrators (stated)

accent, emphasize or reinforce words

18. regulators (stated)

control the back + forth flow of speaking + listening.

19. displays of feelings (stated)

Show through our faces + body

20. jutting

_____

Now compare your answers to the definitions in the word list that follows. Since your definitions are written in your own words, they will probably be less formal and more understandable for you. Check to be sure that the content is essentially the same, but don't substitute the dictionary-type definitions for your own. You will find that learning definitions in your own words rather than memorizing the ones in the book will help you learn the meanings better and remember them longer.

WORD LIST

The words listed below are the ones that you are studying in this chapter. Although you have met them in the context of a communication passage, you may find some of them in other types of textbooks, newspapers, magazines, professional journals, and recreational reading sources as well.

1. **articulation** (ät tik yə lā′ shən), _n._ the process of expressing oneself by using speech organs to pronounce sounds.

2. **competent** (kom′ pə tent), _adj._ capable; fit; qualified for some specific purpose.

3. **display of feelings** (di splā′ uv fēl′ ings) a show of emotion or sensibility through facial expression or body movement.

4. **emblem** (em′ bləm), _n._ **1.** a body movement that has a direct translation into words. **2.** a symbol, as an olive branch as a symbol of peace. **3.** a picture or design that identifies something, as the emblem of a school.

5. **excessively** (ik ses′ iv lē), _adv._ **1.** producing a surplus. **2.** going beyond the usual or expected.

6. **illustrator** (il′ ə strā tər), _n._ **1.** movement or gesture that accents, emphasizes, or reinforces words. **2.** an artist who makes illustrations or pictures.

7. **inappropriate** (in ə prō′ prē it), _adj._ not appropriate, suitable, or proper.

8. **insecure** (in si kyoor′), _adj._ **1.** having doubts; not confident. **2.** not firmly placed. **3.** uncertain.

9. **jutting** (jut′ ing), _adj._ **1.** extending beyond the main body. **2.** projecting or protruding.

10. **kinesics** (ki nē′ siks), *n.* (used with a singular verb) **1.** body movements. **2.** the study of body movements and gestures as a part of communication.

11. **modify** (mod′ ə fī), *v.* **1.** to change somewhat. **2.** grammatically, to describe or limit a particular meaning of another word.

12. **paralanguage** (par′ ə lan′ gwij), *n.* **1.** nonverbal communication. **2.** vocal features that accompany speech and contribute to communication.

13. **perceive** (pər sēv′), *v.* **1.** to recognize or identify. **2.** to become aware of.

14. **pitch** (pich), *n.* **1.** the highness or lowness of a sound. **2.** a dark, sticky, tarlike substance. **3.** the degree of slope, as in a roof. *v.* **4.** to erect a campsite or tent. **5.** to throw or toss. **6.** to attempt to sell something.

15. **quality** (kwol′ ə tē), *n.* **1.** peculiar or essential character. **2.** a characteristic or attribute. **3.** character or nature. **4.** high social status.

16. **regulator** (reg′ yə lā tər), *n.* **1.** a body movement or gesture that controls the flow of a conversation. **2.** a person or thing that regulates, controls, or directs. **3.** a device that controls the flow of liquids.

17. **resonance** (rez′ ə nəns), *n.* **1.** characteristic quality of voiced speech caused by air vibrations in the nose and mouth cavities. **2.** the prolongation of sound, as in an echo. **3.** the amplification of speech sounds.

18. **rhythm** (riTH′ əm), *n.* **1.** the regular rise and fall in the flow of speech. **2.** patterned recurrence of a beat or accent. **3.** a movement or activity that occurs regularly.

19. **tempo** (tem′ pō), *n.* rate of speed of speech, a musical passage, or other activity.

20. **vocal fillers** (vō′ kəl fil′ ərs), *n.* sounds used to fill sentences or allow time to search for words, such as *uh, um, er.*

Exercise 4: Matching

Match the terms in column A with their definitions in column B.

		Column A		*Column B*
ȷ	1.	pitch	a.	capable or qualified
i	2.	vocal fillers	b.	study of body movements
e	3.	insecure	c.	a movement that reinforces words
f	4.	rhythm	d.	a gesture that controls the flow of conversation

_A_ 5.　competent　　　　　　ę. doubtful, lacking confidence

_H_ 6.　paralanguage　　　　　f. rise and fall in the flow of
　　　　　　　　　　　　　　　　speech

_C_ 7.　illustrator　　　　　　g. a body movement that
　　　　　　　　　　　　　　　　translates into words

_d_ 8.　regulator　　　　　　　h. nonverbal communication

_g_ 9.　emblem　　　　　　　　i. sounds used to fill voids

_b_ 10.　kinesics　　　　　　　j. highness or lowness of
　　　　　　　　　　　　　　　　a sound

　　　　　　　　Column A　　　　　　　　*Column B*

_m_ 11.　quality　　　　　　　k. extending or sticking out

_T_ 12.　inappropriate　　　　l. rate of speed of speech

_N_ 13.　resonance　　　　　　m. essential character

_O_ 14.　articulation　　　　　n. vibrating quality of speech

_S_ 15.　excessively　　　　　o. expressing oneself through
　　　　　　　　　　　　　　　　speech

_R_ 16.　display of feelings　p. to change

_P_ 17.　modify　　　　　　　　q. to recognize or identify

_K_ 18.　jutting　　　　　　　r. a show of emotion

_L_ 19.　tempo　　　　　　　　s. producing too much

_Q_ 20.　perceive　　　　　　　t. not suitable

Exercise 5: Fill-In

Choose the word that best completes each sentence below and write its letter in the space provided.

a. illustrator　　d. articulation　　g. paralanguage　i. resonance
b. vocal fillers　e. emblem　　　　h. regulators　　j. pitch
c. kinesics　　　f. display of feelings

_b_ 1.　When delivering a speech in front of the class, nervous
　　　　students often use vocalfillers to give them time to collect
　　　　their thoughts.

_g_ 2. President Clinton is noted for his public _____ that make his speeches seem more emotional on camera than in the newspaper.

_e_ 3. The fisherman used an ~~Amesic~~ to reinforce the impressive size of his fish.

_a_ 4. Counseling psychologists often pay as much attention to Kinesics as to the words of their clients.

_____ 5. Chairpersons use _____ to grant permission to speak, to halt interruptions, and to cut off lengthy comments.

_____ 6. Even though his English was limited, the foreign exchange student was able to secure rides by using the _____ of extending his thumb.

_____ 7. Movie producers rely on _____ to gauge a preview audience's reaction to a new film.

_____ 8. As the customer grew more upset, the store manager noticed the _____ of her voice rise.

_____ 9. Because of her clear _____, the police dispatcher's instructions were rarely misunderstood.

_____ 10. As he prepared for a major role in a Shakespearean play, Charles' drama coach helped him develop _____ so he could be heard at the rear of the auditorium.

Exercise 6: Application

Briefly describe a conversation between a student and her professor. In addition to telling the topic of the conversation, describe how nonverbal communication on the part of a student may lead the professor to form an impression of him or her.

_____

_____

_____

_____

_____

_____

ACCOUNTING: CAREERS IN ACCOUNTING

2

This chapter deals with the accounting profession. You will read about careers in the accounting field and learn some vocabulary words that will help your understanding. First you will read an excerpt from an accounting textbook. Some of the terms in the reading will be numbered and underlined. Your first task will be to define them either from context or from the stated definition. In the exercises that follow, you will practice using the terms.

Accounting is a profession that interests many students. Those who enjoy math or found that they did well in a high school bookkeeping class are often attracted to accounting. Those who enjoy the logic of analysis may be intrigued with the role of the accountant as a financial or business advisor. And those who are practical may look forward to the profession's high salaries and job availability.

Read the following selection about careers in accounting to learn about the choices available in this profession.

CAREERS IN ACCOUNTING

The Accounting "Profession"

Accounting—along with such fields as architecture, engineering, law, medicine, and theology—is recognized as a "profession." What distinguishes a (1) profession from other disciplines? There is no widely recognized definition of a profession, but all these fields have several characteristics in common.

First, all professions involve a complex and (2) evolving body of knowledge. In accounting, the (3) complexity and the ever-changing nature of the business world, financial reporting requirements, and income tax laws certainly meet this (4) criterion.

In all professions, (5) practitioners must use their professional judgment to resolve many problems and (6) dilemmas. Throughout this text, we will point out situations requiring accountants to exercise professional judgment.

Of greatest importance, however, is the unique responsibility of professionals *to serve the public's best interest, even at the sacrifice of personal advantage.* This responsibility stems from the fact that the public has little technical knowledge in the professions, yet fair and competent performance by professionals is (7) vital to the public's health, safety, or well-being. The practice of medicine, for example, directly affects public health, while engineering affects public safety. Accounting affects the public's well-being in many ways, because accounting information is used in the (8) allocation of economic resources throughout society. Thus, accountants have a basic "social contract" to avoid being associated with misleading information.

Accountants tend to specialize in specific fields, as do the members of other professions. In terms of career opportunities, accounting may be divided into four broad areas: (a) public accounting, (b) managerial accounting, (c) governmental accounting, and (d) accounting education.

Public Accounting

Certified public accountants, called CPAs, offer a variety of accounting services to the public. These individuals may work in a CPA firm, or as sole practitioners.

The work of CPAs consists primarily of (9) <u>auditing</u> financial statements, income tax work, and (10) <u>management advisory services</u> (management consulting). Some CPAs also offer bookkeeping services to small businesses, but many do not.

Providing management advisory services is, perhaps, the fastest-growing area in public accounting. The advisory services extend well beyond tax planning and accounting matters; CPAs advise management on such diverse issues as international (11) <u>mergers</u>, manufacturing processes, and the introduction of new products. The entry of CPAs into the field of management consulting reflects the fact that *financial considerations enter into almost every business decision.*

A great many CPAs move from public accounting into managerial positions with their client organizations. These "alumni" from public accounting often move directly into such top management positions as controller, treasurer, chief financial officer, or chief executive officer.

Managerial Accounting

In contrast to the CPA who serves many clients, the managerial (or management) accountant works for one (12) <u>enterprise</u>. Managerial accountants develop and interpret accounting information designed specifically to meet the various needs of management.

The chief accounting officer of an organization usually is called the (13) **<u>controller</u>,** in recognition of the fact that one basic purpose of accounting data is to aid in controlling business operations. The controller is part of the top management team, which is responsible for running the business, setting its objectives, and seeing that these objectives are achieved.

In addition to developing information to assist managers, managerial accountants are responsible for operating the company's accounting system, including the recording of (14) <u>transactions</u> and the preparation of financial statements, tax returns, and other accounting reports.

Governmental Accounting

Governmental agencies use accounting information in allocating their resources and in controlling their operations. Therefore, the need for management accountants is similar to that in business organizations.

In addition, the government performs several specialized audit functions.

The GAO: Who Audits the Government? The General Accounting Office (GAO) audits many agencies of the federal government, and also some private organizations doing business with the government. The GAO reports its findings directly to Congress. Congress, in turn, often (15) <u>discloses</u> these findings to the public.

GAO investigations may be designed either to evaluate the efficiency of an (16) <u>entity</u>'s operations, or to determine the fairness of accounting information reported to the government.

The IRS: Audits of Income Tax Returns Another governmental agency that performs extensive auditing work is the Internal Revenue Service (IRS). The IRS handles the millions of income tax returns filed annually by individuals and business organizations, and frequently performs auditing functions to verify (17) <u>data</u> contained in these returns.

The SEC: The "Watchdog" of Financial Reporting The SEC works closely with the FASB (Financial Accounting Standards Board) in establishing generally accepted accounting principles. Each year large publicly owned corporations must file audited financial statements with the SEC. If the SEC believes that a company's financial statements are (18) <u>deficient</u> in any way, it conducts an investigation. If the SEC concludes that federal securities laws have been violated, it initiates legal action against the reporting entity and responsible individuals.

Many other governmental agencies, including the FBI, the Treasury Department, and the FDIC (Federal Deposit Insurance Corporation), use accountants to audit (19) <u>compliance</u> with government regulations and to investigate suspected criminal activity. People beginning their careers in governmental accounting often move into top administrative positions.

Accounting Education

Many accountants, including your instructor and the authors of this textbook, have chosen to (20) <u>pursue</u> careers in accounting education. A position as an accounting faculty member offers opportunities for research and consulting, and an unusual degree of freedom in developing individual skills. Accounting educators contribute to the accounting profession in many ways. One, of course, lies in effective teaching; another, in publishing significant research findings; and a third, in influencing top students to pursue careers in accounting.

Exercise 1: Summary

Before you begin to zero in on the underlined words in the passage, try to talk with a fellow student about the content of the passage. Then, in your own words, write a brief summary of what you have learned about careers in accounting. Include some specific details about what accountants do.

_____

_____

_____

_____

_____

Exercise 2: Example

Give an example of a situation in which someone might consult an accountant, and tell which type of accountant to consult.

_____

_____

_____

_____

Exercise 3: Definitions

Working on your own or with a fellow student, try to define the underlined words from the selection you have just read. In many cases, you can find the definition in the text. The notation "(stated)" will tell you when this is so. For other terms, you will need to rely on the context and your own background knowledge. Write each definition in the space provided after the word.

1. profession (stated)

    _____

2. evolving

    _____

3. complexity

    _____

4. criterion

    _____

5. practitioners

    _____

6. dilemmas

    _____

7. vital

_____

8. allocation

_____

9. auditing

_____

10. management advisory services (stated)

_____

11. mergers

_____

12. enterprise

_____

13. controller (stated)

_____

14. transactions

_____

15. discloses

_____

16. entity

_____

17. data

_____

18. deficient

_____

19. compliance

_____

20. pursue

_____

Now compare your answers to the definitions in the word list that follows. Since your definitions are written in your own words, they will probably be less formal and more understandable for you. Check to be sure that the content is essentially the same, but don't substitute the dictionary-type definitions for your own. You will find that learning definitions in your own words rather than memorizing the ones in the book will help you learn the meanings better and remember them longer.

WORD LIST

The words listed below are the ones that you are studying in this chapter. Although you have met them in the context of an accounting passage, you may find some of them in other types of textbooks, newspapers, magazines, professional journals, and recreational reading sources as well.

1. **allocation** (al ə kā′ shən), *n.* **1.** the act of setting aside for a particular purpose. **2.** allotment or the share being distributed. **3.** portion.

2. **audit** (ô′ dit), *n.* **1.** a formal examination and verification of financial records. **2.** a report detailing the audit. *v.* **3.** to perform a financial examination. **4.** to investigate something's efficiency, as *an energy audit.* **5.** to attend a course without expecting credit.

3. **complexity** (kəm pleks′ ə tē), *n.* **1.** the state of being composed of many parts. **2.** the quality of being hard to analyze or solve.

4. **compliance** (kəm plī′ əns), *n.* **1.** the act of conforming or yielding to a demand or proposal. **2.** a tendency to yield easily to others. **3.** obedience or cooperation.

5. **controller** (kən trō′ lər), *n.* **1.** the chief accounting officer of an organization. **2.** a person that regulates or controls. **3.** a mechanical device that regulates.

6. **criterion** (krī tēr′ ē ən), *n.* pl. *criteria.* a standard of judgment; a rule for evaluation.

7. **data** (dā′ tə, dat′ ə), *n.* pl. of *datum.* factual information or statistics.

8. **deficient** (di fish′ ənt), *adj.* **1.** lacking something necessary. **2.** defective.

9. **dilemma** (di lem′ ə), *n.* **1.** a choice between undesirable alternatives. **2.** a perplexing situation or problem.

10. **disclose** (dis klōz), *v.* **1.** to reveal. **2.** to expose to view.

11. **enterprise** (en′ tər prīz), *n.* **1.** undertaking or project. **2.** boldness or readiness for daring action. **3.** a company organized for commercial purposes; business firm.

12. **entity** (en′ ti tē), *n.* **1.** something that exists as a distinct, independent unit. **2.** something that has existence or being.

13. **evolving** (ē volv′ ing), *v.* developing or changing gradually.

14. **management advisory service** (man ij′ ment ad vī′ zə rē sər′ vis) consultation and recommendations about controlling and directing an enterprise or business.

15. **merger** (mər′ jər), *n.* a combination of two or more companies; a takeover of a corporation by another.

16. **practitioner** (prak tish′ ə nər), *n.* one who is engaged in the practice of a profession.

17. **profession** (prə fesh′ ən), *n.* **1.** a vocation requiring education and training. **2.** the body of people engaged in the same occupation. **3.** a declaration of belief or faith.

18. **pursue** (pər soo′), *v.* **1.** to strive to accomplish. **2.** to engage in a career. **3.** to follow with the intent to overtake or capture.

19. **transaction** (tran zak′ shən), *n.* something conducted or carried on, as a business deal.

20. **vital** (vīt′ l), *adj.* **1.** necessary to life. **2.** energetic, animated, or lively.

Exercise 4: Matching

Match the terms in column A with their definitions in column B.

	Column A	Column B
_____ 1.	merger	a. the quality of being difficult to figure out
_____ 2.	dilemma	b. a business deal
_____ 3.	allocation	c. chief accounting officer
_____ 4.	enterprise	d. combination of companies
_____ 5.	transaction	e. a career requiring education
_____ 6.	data	f. an undertaking or project
_____ 7.	evolving	g. portion or allotment
_____ 8.	complexity	h. a problem situation
_____ 9.	controller	i. information
_____ 10.	profession	j. changing gradually

	Column A	Column B
_____ 11.	pursue	k. one engaged in a profession
_____ 12.	disclose	l. to examine financial records
_____ 13.	entity	m. lacking something
_____ 14.	compliance	n. an independent unit
_____ 15.	vital	o. to engage in a career
_____ 16.	practitioner	p. to reveal
_____ 17.	criterion	q. cooperation or obedience
_____ 18.	deficient	r. consultation and recommendation
_____ 19.	audit	s. necessary
_____ 20.	management advisory services	t. standard

Exercise 5: Fill-In

Choose the word that best completes each sentence below and write its letter in the space provided.

a. transaction   d. enterprise   g. audit   i. compliance
b. allocation   e. merger   h. management   j. data
c. controller   f. profession   advisory services

_____ 1. Many companies carry on both internal and external

_____s of their records to ensure their accuracy and integrity.

_____ 2. Employees of the electronics company worried that the

_____ with their former competitor would result in the loss of jobs.

_____ 3. The new _____ insisted that he be consulted about any purchases that exceeded $1,000.

_____ 4. After retiring from IBM, the former vice president set up his

own firm offering _____ to start-up companies that might benefit from his expertise.

_____ 5. The bankruptcy officer issued strict orders about the

_____ of the remaining funds among the creditors.

_____ 6. After analyzing the _____ , the accountant
recommended that his client borrow money to expand his
growing car repair business.

_____ 7. After signing the contract, the seller was allowed 30 days to

complete the _____ by delivering the product in good
condition.

_____ 8. Some cities have designated _____ zones where new
businesses are offered incentives such as tax credits if they
locate there.

_____ 9. Many _____s, like medicine and accounting, require
licensing exams before an individual is certified to practice.

_____ 10. The paper company would be fined $500 a day until

it was in _____ with the state's new environmental
regulations.

Exercise 6: Application

Tell a friend the different opportunities available in the accounting field.
Explain the differences among careers in public accounting, managerial
accounting, governmental accounting, and accounting education.

_____

_____

_____

_____

_____

Biology: Development, Aging, and Senescence— Changes over the Life Span

3

Biology is usually regarded as a challenging subject that requires careful reading and study. College students who have not studied biology in high school may either take a preparatory course or expect to put a lot of time into learning the terminology and concepts. Many students find biology a fascinating subject, particularly as they learn more about the human body. Students interested in becoming nurses, doctors, physical therapists, laboratory technicians, or physical education teachers will find themselves in biology classes. Science majors, of course, will study biology, too.

The excerpt in this chapter from a biology book gives a brief overview of the changes that take place as an individual moves through various life-stage changes. In a typical biology textbook, a passage like this one would serve as an introduction or overview to a chapter. Later in the chapter, you would read about each life stage in more detail. Such an introduction also presents some of the vocabulary you will encounter throughout the chapter. Passages like this one often seem very dense because a lot of information is presented at once. If you regard it as an outline or a preview of what is to come, you will not feel overwhelmed. Concentrate on learning the terminology at the beginning. Then, when you meet those words in a larger context later on, the vocabulary and the content will work together to enhance your understanding of the material.

Read the following selection about changes over the life span to learn something about how our bodies change as we age.

DEVELOPMENT, AGING, AND SENESCENCE: CHANGES OVER THE LIFE SPAN

It is convenient to divide the (1) <u>life span</u> into three stages: embryological development, growth and maturation, and adulthood. (2) **Embryological development** occurs between the time of (3) <u>fertilization</u> and the time of birth. During this 38-week period, cells (4) <u>proliferate</u> and undergo (5) <u>profound</u> changes. They acquire specialized functions, allowing tissues, organs, and systems to form.

Growth and (6) <u>**maturation**</u> encompasses the periods of infancy, childhood, adolescence, and early adulthood (from birth to the mid-twenties). This is a dramatic stage of the life span. There are increases in body size and height and great changes in the structure and functions of tissues. The body becomes capable of reproduction (7) (<u>puberty</u>) during this stage, and many human qualities are acquired by learning: reasoning ability, use of language, moral judgment, and social interaction, to name a few. In spite of growth and change, there is a general decline in the *rate of growth* during this stage.

We enter (8) <u>adulthood</u> when growth in height (9) <u>ceases</u>. Adulthood is marked by a (10) <u>sustained</u> capacity of the body to repair and maintain itself. However, significant changes occur in some organs and systems during this period. For example, the thymus gland decreases in size after helping to establish the body's (11) <u>immune</u> defenses. Late adulthood is associated with a decline in these defensive, repair, and maintenance (12) <u>capacities</u>.

If we exclude the body changes associated with illness and healing, we can distinguish three different kinds of changes that take place in the human body: developmental changes, aging changes, and senescence.

Developmental changes produce a full-grown and sexually mature male or female who is capable of independence and a social life. These changes are dramatically evident from (13) <u>conception</u> to maturity 20 years later.

Aging involves what usually are slow changes in the structure and function of the body, (14) <u>altering</u> one's appearance and reducing one's capacity to survive. Aging is a natural process that begins very early in the life of an individual. Usually the aging process is slow, (15) <u>progressive</u>, and (16) <u>cumulative</u>, and people do not experience (17) <u>incapacity</u> until late in the life span. Severe incapacity associated with the end of the life span is called senescence. (18) **Senescence** involves a reduced capacity of the body to defend itself, repair itself, and maintain constant internal conditions. **Death** is marked by the complete inability of the body to regulate and maintain itself.

Aging shows a great deal of variation. Over the entire life span, the rate of aging is not uniform within the same individual or between individuals. If we could watch the different organs of one person over time and (19) monitor the changes that occur, we would find that each organ ages at a different rate. The "biological" age of an organ is therefore not necessarily the same as the (20) chronological age of an individual. In humans, the rate of aging is influenced by genetic, psychological, social and economic factors.

Exercise 1: Summary

Before you begin to zero in on the underlined words in the passage, try to talk with a fellow student about the content of the passage. Then, in your own words, write a brief summary of what you have learned about human development. Include some specific details about the three different stages of the life span.

_____

_____

_____

_____

_____

Exercise 2: Example

Using yourself (or someone you know), identify your (or someone else's) current life stage and tell what characterizes it.

_____

_____

_____

_____

Exercise 3: Definitions

Working on your own or with a fellow student, try to define the underlined words from the selection you have just read. In many cases, you can find the definition in the text. The notation "(stated)" will tell you when this is so. For other terms, you will need to rely on the context and your own background knowledge. Write each definition in the space provided after the word.

1. life span

   _____

2. embryological development (stated)

   _____

3. fertilization

   _____

4. proliferate

   _____

5. profound

   _____

6. maturation (stated)

   _____

7. puberty (stated)

   _____

8. adulthood (stated)

   _____

9. ceases

   _____

10. sustained

    _____

11. immune

    _____

12. capacities

    _____

13. conception

_____

14. altering

_____

15. progressive

_____

16. cumulative

_____

17. incapacity

_____

18. senescence (stated)

_____

19. monitor

_____

20. chronological

_____

Now compare your answers to the definitions in the word list that follows.
Since your definitions are written in your own words, they will probably be
less formal and more understandable for you. Check to be sure that the content is essentially the same, but don't substitute the dictionary-type definitions for your own. You will find that learning definitions in your own
words rather than memorizing the ones in the book will help you learn the
meanings better and remember them longer.

WORD LIST

The words listed below are the ones that you are studying in this chapter.
Although you have met them in the context of a biology passage, you may
find some of them in other types of textbooks, newspapers, magazines, professional journals, and recreational reading sources as well.

1. **adulthood** (ə dult′ hûd), _n._ **1.** the state in which growth in height ceases and
   the body has a sustained capacity to repair and maintain itself. **2.** the state of
   being fully developed and mature.

2. **altering** (ôl′ tər ing), *v.* changing; making different in some way.

3. **capacities** (kə pas i tēz), *n. pl.* **1.** actual or potential abilities to perform. **2.** legal qualification or fitness. **3.** the ability to receive or contain. **4.** the maximum number that can be contained.

4. **cease** (sēs), *v.* to come to an end; to stop.

5. **chronological** (krən i loj′ ik əl), *adj.* arranged in order of occurrence in time.

6. **conception** (kən sep′ shən), *n.* **1.** the act of fertilization. **2.** a notion, idea, or concept.

7. **cumulative** (kyoo′ myə lə tiv), *adj.* increasing by successive additions.

8. **embryological development** (em brē ə loj′ i kəl di vel′ up ment), the growth and change that occurs between the time of fertilization and birth.

9. **fertilization** (fərt′ l ə zā shən), *n.* **1.** the process of joining an egg with a sperm to make it capable of development. **2.** the act of impregnating. **3.** the enrichment of soil.

10. **immune** (im myoon′), *adj.* **1.** pertaining to the production of antibodies. **2.** protected from a disease. **3.** exempt.

11. **incapacity** (in kə pas′ i tē), *n.* lacking ability, strength, or qualification.

12. **life span** (līf span), *n.* **1.** the longest period over which the life of any organism might extend. **2.** the length, duration, or longevity of an individual life.

13. **maturation** (ma chə rā′ shən), *n.* the act or process of becoming mature or fully developed.

14. **monitor** (mon′ i tər), *v.* **1.** to watch, check, or observe. *n.* **2.** a student assigned to assist a teacher. **3.** a video display as for a computer or television.

15. **profound** (prə found′), *adj.* **1.** significant. **2.** marked by depth or insight. **3.** complete and pervasive.

16. **progressive** (prə gres′ iv), *adj.* **1.** going forward or onward, passing from one stage to the next. **2.** advancing. **3.** advocating political or social reform.

17. **proliferate** (prə lif′ ə rāt), *v.* to grow, spread, or increase rapidly, as by cell division.

18. **puberty** (pyoo′ bər tē), *n.* the state or condition when an individual first becomes capable of reproduction.

19. **senescence** (si nes′ ens), *n.* the state of being old that includes a reduced capacity of the body to defend and repair itself, and to maintain constant internal conditions.

20. **sustained** (sus tānd′) *v.* **1.** keeping going; maintained. **2.** supported; held up. **3.** held as true.

Exercise 4: Matching

Match the terms in column A with their definitions in column B.

	Column A	Column B
_____ 1.	puberty	a. lacking ability or strength
_____ 2.	progressive	b. the joining of an egg and sperm
_____ 3.	monitor	c. stop
_____ 4.	immune	d. duration of life
_____ 5.	fertilization	e. the stage at which reproduction is possible
_____ 6.	life span	f. to observe or check
_____ 7.	altering	g. producing antibodies
_____ 8.	profound	h. advancing through stages
_____ 9.	cease	i. changing
_____ 10.	incapacity	j. significant

	Column A	Column B
_____ 11.	conception	k. growth between fertilization and birth
_____ 12.	chronological	l. period of old age
_____ 13.	capacities	m. period of full or completed growth
_____ 14.	embryological development	n. arranged in time sequence
_____ 15.	cumulative	o. process of growth and development
_____ 16.	proliferate	p. fertilization
_____ 17.	adulthood	q. continued or supported
_____ 18.	senescence	r. potential abilities
_____ 19.	maturation	s. to increase or multiply
_____ 20.	sustained	t. increasing by additions

Exercise 5: Fill-In

Choose the word that best completes each sentence below and write its letter in the space provided.

a. puberty
b. senescence
c. life span

d. embryological development
e. immune

f. maturation
g. adulthood
h. fertilization

i. progressive
j. chronological

_____ 1. The use of alcohol and tobacco during pregnancy has a negative effect on the _____ of the fetus.

_____ 2. Many Americans end their days in nursing homes because of the consequences associated with _____.

_____ 3. Good nutrition, sanitary conditions, and modern medicine have an effect on the average _____, which varies from one part of the world to another.

_____ 4. The pathologist estimated that the _____ age of the corpse was between 18 and 25 years old.

_____ 5. Sex education should precede the onset of _____.

_____ 6. Believing herself _____ to poison ivy, Stella spent hours in her garden pulling out the vine.

_____ 7. After Maria tried unsuccessfully for several years to become pregnant, her doctor prescribed medication to increase the chances of _____.

_____ 8. Even when their children have reached _____, some parents find it difficult to refrain from trying to run their lives.

_____ 9. Growth and _____ are influenced by heredity and diet.

_____ 10. When Roberto's parents learned that he was suffering from a _____ disease, they started to make long-term provisions for his care.

Exercise 6: Application

Describe how the process of aging has affected someone you know.

_____

_____

_____

_____

_____

SOCIOLOGY: FAMILY FUNCTIONS AND STRUCTURE

4

Sociology is the study of people in groups. We choose some of the groups we belong to and are assigned to others. One very important group in any society is the family. Different individuals and cultures have their own notions of what constitutes a family. In the passage you will read, you will learn something about what purposes a family serves (functions) and how families are organized (structure). Some of the families described are quite different from the typical American family (if there even is such a thing).

College students majoring in liberal arts study sociology as part of their social science requirement. History, economics, and psychology also are part of the discipline known as the social sciences. Students who are interested in working as social workers often major in sociology as undergraduates and continue to study for a master's degree in the field. Others may wish to engage in sociological research, examining patterns and trends that may be peculiar to a certain cultural group.

Read the following selection to learn what a family is, what it does for its members, and how it is organized.

FAMILY FUNCTIONS AND STRUCTURE

A (1) **family** is any group of people who are united by ties of marriage, (2) <u>ancestry</u>, or adoption, especially those having the responsibility for rearing children. In some form the family is part of the social organization in all societies. Indeed, it is probably the most basic of all social institutions.

Functions of the Family

The family is considered so important because it responds to some of the most fundamental human needs, both individual and (3) <u>collective</u>.

- The *need for love and emotional security:* The family involves a set of "loving obligations" to share both material and emotional (4) <u>resources</u>. Ideally, the family offers warmth, loyalty, concern, willingness to sacrifice for the good of others, and unconditional love. . . .

- The *need to regulate sexual behavior:* All societies place limits on the sexual behavior of their members, including limits regarding who can have sexual relations with whom. Forbidding sex between family members related by close common descent (called the [5] <u>incest taboo)</u> is a universal restriction.

- The *need to produce new generations:* At the same time, the family fulfills the *need to* (6) *socialize children.* Children are society's (7) "<u>raw recruits</u>." They must be taught the elements of culture needed for competent participation in social life. The family is the primary arena for social learning.

- The *need to protect the young and the* (8) *<u>disabled</u>:* During infancy and early childhood, humans are dependent on their parents for food, clothing, shelter, and basic care. Even as adults, many people experience episodes of illness or disability during which they need help. The family sees its members through these times.

- The *need to "place" people in the social order:* The structure of a society is an (9) <u>intricate web</u> of social roles and statuses. People must somehow be placed within these statuses and motivated to play the appropriate roles. Even in the United States and other societies that stress equal opportunity and social mobility, people's (10) <u>ascribed</u>

statuses, including their national, (11) ethnic, racial, religious, class, and community identities, derive largely from family membership.

Variations in Family Structure

The family functions just listed are common to all societies. The structural forms for fulfilling these functions, however, vary from one society to another. Most people think their way of organizing family life is not only morally right but natural. Only the basics of procreation are determined by biology, however; the rest varies from culture to culture. Male dominance is among the most widespread features of family life, but even its extent and form varies, as the following examples suggest.

- To the Nayar of Kerala, India, it is natural for a woman's brother—rather than the children's biological father—to share in the raising of her children. During adolescence, a Nayar girl is encouraged to have several lovers. If she becomes pregnant, one or more of these lovers acknowledges (12) paternity and pays the cost of delivery. Beyond this, however, none of the lovers has any obligations toward the girl or the child. The girl's (13) kin are responsible for caring for her and the baby. Property and privileged status pass not from father to son but from mother's brother to nephew. . . .

- Among the Betsileo of Madagascar, a man is allowed to have several wives. Each wife is housed in the village adjoining one of the rice fields that the man owns. Wealthier men with more rice fields can support more wives. The first and most senior wife, called the *big wife*, lives in the village next to the best, most productive rice field. The husband lives mainly with this woman but visits the others as he oversees his other fields. . . .

- In the foothills of the western Himalayas, brothers share a wife. The oldest brother arranges the marriage, and his brothers become co-husbands, with all of them living together in a single household. Any children the wife bears call all the brothers "father." The brothers are free as a group to marry additional women if they wish, in which case all the wives are shared by all the husbands. . . .

Social scientists have categorized such variations in family structure using a number of criteria, one of which is the number of partners involved in a marriage. Both culturally and legally, U.S. society advocates (14) **monogamy,** marriage between one man and one woman. Other societies permit (15) **polygamy,** marriage involving more than two partners at the same time. When a man has more than one wife at the same time, it is known as (16) **polygyny.** Much less common is (17) **polyandry,** in which a woman has more than one husband at the same time.

Another structural criterion is the degree of importance given to marital ties, as opposed to blood ties. When marital ties are paramount, a husband and wife and their immature children form a core unit, called the (18) **nuclear family.** This arrangement is the traditional structure in the United States and in most other modern Western countries. It also exists in somewhat different forms in other societies, such as the Betsileo, in which a man may establish several nuclear families in separate villages. Of course, multiple marriages are not required for a person to belong to more than one nuclear family. In the United States, for example, most people are eventually members of two nuclear families. The first, called the (19) **family of orientation,** consists of parents and siblings. The second, called the (20) **family of procreation,** consists of one's spouse and children.

Exercise 1: Summary

Before you begin to zero in on the underlined words in the passage, try to talk with a fellow student about the content of the passage. Then, in your own words, write a brief summary of what you have learned about the functions of families. Include some specific details about what families do for their members.

_____

_____

_____

_____

_____

Exercise 2: Example

Describe the family group you live in and tell what term in the passage you would use to describe or characterize it.

_____

_____

_____

_____

Exercise 3: Definitions

Working on your own or with a fellow student, try to define the underlined words from the selection you have just read. In many cases, you can find the definition in the text. The notation "(stated)" will tell you when this is so. For other terms, you will need to rely on the context and your own background knowledge. Write each definition in the space provided after the word.

1. family (stated)

   _____

2. ancestry

   _____

3. collective

   _____

4. resources

   _____

5. incest taboo (stated)

   _____

6. socialize

   _____

7. raw recruits

   _____

8. disabled

   _____

9. intricate web

   _____

10. ascribed statuses

    _____

11. ethnic

    _____

12. paternity

    _____

13. kin

_____

14. monogamy (stated)

_____

15. polygamy (stated)

_____

16. polygyny (stated)

_____

17. polyandry (stated)

_____

18. nuclear family (stated)

_____

19. family of orientation (stated)

_____

20. family of procreation (stated)

_____

Now compare your answers to the definitions in the word list that follows. Since your definitions are written in your own words, they will probably be less formal and more understandable for you. Check to be sure that the content is essentially the same, but don't substitute the dictionary-type definitions for your own. You will find that learning definitions in your own words rather than memorizing the ones in the book will help you learn the meanings better and remember them longer.

WORD LIST

The words listed below are the ones that you are studying in this chapter. Although you have met them in the context of a sociology passage, you may find some of them in other types of textbooks, newspapers, magazines, professional journals, and recreational reading sources as well.

1. **ancestry** (an′ ses trē), _n._ **1.** line of descent, lineage. **2.** the origin of an idea. **3.** the history of a style or practice.

2. **ascribed status** (ə scrībd sta′ təs) the social position assigned to a person on the basis of age, sex, race, etc.

3. **collective** (kə lek′ tiv), *adj.* **1.** relating to members of a group as a whole. **2.** involving all members of a group, as opposed to individuals.

4. **disabled** (dis ā′ bld), *adj.* incapacitated by illness; mentally or physically handicapped.

5. **ethnic** (eth′ nik), *adj.* relating to a group of people that share a common culture, religion, or language.

6. **family** (fam′ lē), *n.* any group of people who are united by marriage, ancestry, or adoption, especially those with the responsibility of rearing children.

7. **family of orientation** (fam′ lē əv ôr ē ən tā′ shən) a nuclear family that consists of one's parents and siblings.

8. **family of procreation** (fam′ lē əv prō krē ā′ shən) a nuclear family consisting of one's spouse and children.

9. **incest taboo** (in′ sest tə bōō′) the prohibition of sex between family members related by close common descent.

10. **intricate web** (in′ tri kət web) a complicated set or pattern of circumstances.

11. **kin** (kin), *n.* an individual's relatives; a group of persons from a common ancestor constituting a family, race, clan, or tribe.

12. **monogamy** (mə nog′ ə mē), *n.* marriage between one man and one woman; having only one spouse at a time.

13. **nuclear family** (nōōk′ lē ər fam′ lē) a core social unit consisting of a mother, father, and children.

14. **paternity** (pə tər′ nə tē), *n.* fatherhood; the state of being a father.

15. **polyandry** (pol′ ē an drē), *n.* the practice of having more than one husband at a time.

16. **polygamy** (pə lig′ ə mē), *n.* marriage involving more than two partners.

17. **polygyny** (pə lij′ ə nē), *n.* the practice of having more than one wife at a time.

18. **raw recruits** (rô ri krōōtz′) inexperienced or untrained members of a group.

19. **resources** (rē sors′ iz), *n. pl.* **1.** available means. **2.** sources of supply or support. **3.** abilities to meet and handle situations.

20. **socialize** (sō′ shəl īz), *v.* to make social; to adapt for life in the company of others.

Exercise 4: Matching

Match the terms in column A with their definitions in column B.

	Column A	Column B
_____ 1.	raw recruits	a. a group of people united by marriage or ancestry
_____ 2.	intricate web	b. relatives
_____ 3.	polygamy	c. marriage involving more than two partners
_____ 4.	family	d. family group of one's parents and siblings
_____ 5.	collective	e. untrained group members
_____ 6.	incest taboo	f. pertaining to a group that shares a common culture or race
_____ 7.	family of orientation	g. marriage to more than one husband
_____ 8.	kin	h. prohibition of sex between close relatives
_____ 9.	polyandry	i. complicated framework
_____ 10.	ethnic	j. relating to a group

	Column A	Column B
_____ 11.	disabled	k. lineage or descent
_____ 12.	resources	l. family group of one's spouse and children
_____ 13.	paternity	m. marriage to one spouse at a time
_____ 14.	ascribed status	n. incapacitated
_____ 15.	nuclear family	o. fatherhood
_____ 16.	monogamy	p. a core social unit with adults and children
_____ 17.	polygyny	q. a source of supply or support
_____ 18.	ancestry	r. marriage to more than one wife

_____ 19.	family of procreation	s. to train for living with others
_____ 20.	socialize	t. assigned social position based on race, sex, age, etc.

Exercise 5: Fill-In

Choose the word that best completes each sentence below and write its letter in the space provided.

a. resources   d. kin   g. ancestry   i. paternity
b. raw recruits   e. disabled   h. ethnic   j. intricate web
c. collective   f. socialize

_____ 1. The tribe assumed _____ responsibility for raising the children whose parents had been killed in the landslide.

_____ 2. In spite of her royal _____, the princess was forced to live a life of poverty after her family was exiled from the country.

_____ 3. Efforts to _____ the child who had been brought up in a hunting camp were unsuccessful, and he left the city after a few weeks.

_____ 4. Calling upon limited emotional and financial _____, the townspeople tried to rebuild after the flood.

_____ 5. After a brief stay in Atlanta, Lucy returned to her _____ in Alabama and worked on the family farm.

_____ 6. Lawyers charged that the _____ suit was without merit, and that the young woman's claim that the popular actor was her father was without merit.

_____ 7. At the beginning of the season, the football coach intimidated and harassed the _____ to see how they reacted under pressure.

_____ 8. Federal laws guarantee that _____ individuals have access to public buildings, an education, and job opportunities.

_____ 9. Patrick journeyed to Ireland to see the country of his great grandparents and to try to trace his _____ through local town records.

_____ 10. In trying to immigrate to the United States and apply for citizenship,

Manuel faced an _____ of application forms and procedures.

Exercise 6: Application

Families are characterized by the number of partners involved in a marriage. Explain why you think the U.S. culture advocates monogamy and give your opinion on the practice.

_____

_____

_____

_____

_____

HISTORY: EQUAL RIGHTS FOR WOMEN

5

In this chapter, you will read some history and learn some vocabulary words that will help you to understand it. First you will read an excerpt from a history textbook. Some of the terms in the reading will be numbered and underlined. Your first task will be to define. In the following exercises, you will practice using the terms.

History provides us with an account of events that occurred before we were alive. It provides us with some perspective about the period we live in. An analysis of what has happened in the past can often help us predict the future or try to change the course of events. History tells our story—*his story* and *her story*. The passage you will read in this chapter tells about changes in women's rights from colonial times to the present. Many students regard the women's movement as a relatively modern occurrence. History tells us that some women were dissatisfied with their status and restrictions centuries ago. The last half of the eighteenth century can be called an age of reformers. Many activists worked for change in various aspects of society. One group consisted of those who thought women should be able to vote, own property, receive an education, pursue a career, and be treated as equal to men in divorce and other legal proceedings. In 1848, a meeting took place at Seneca Falls during which a declaration of women's rights was drafted, many of whose principles are just as relevant today.

Read the following selection about women's rights to learn something about the gains women have made and the way they came about.

EQUAL RIGHTS: STRUGGLING TOWARD FAIRNESS

WOMEN

The United States carried over from English common law a political (1) <u>disregard</u> for women, forbidding them to vote, hold public office, and serve on juries. Upon marriage, a woman (2) <u>essentially</u> lost her identity as an individual and could not own and (3) <u>dispose</u> of property without her husband's (4) <u>consent</u>. Even the wife's body was not fully hers. A wife's adultery was ruled by the Supreme Court to be a (5) <u>violation</u> of the husband's property rights! The first women's rights convention in America was held in 1848 in Seneca Falls, New York, after Lucretia Mott and Elizabeth Cady Stanton had been (6) <u>barred</u> from the main floor of an antislavery convention. Thereafter, however, the struggle for women's rights became closely (7) <u>aligned</u> with the (8) <u>abolitionist</u> movement, but the passage of the post–Civil War constitutional amendments proved to be a setback for the women's movement. The Fifteenth Amendment, for example, said that the right to vote could not be (9) <u>abridged</u> on account of race or color, but said nothing about sex. After decades of struggle, the Nineteenth Amendment was finally adopted in 1920, forbidding denial of the right to vote "by the United States or by any state on account of sex."

Women's Legal and Political Gains

In 1923 women's leaders proposed another constitutional (10) <u>amendment</u>, one that would guarantee equal rights for women. After numerous failed attempts to gain congressional approval, the Equal Rights Amendment (ERA) was passed by Congress in 1973 and went to the state legislatures for (11) <u>ratification</u>. The ERA failed to gain the support of a legislative majority in the thirty-eight states needed for ratification. The proposed amendment was three states short when the deadline for ratification arrived in 1982.

Although the ERA did not become part of the Constitution, it helped bring women's rights to the (12) <u>forefront</u> at a time when developments in Congress and the courts were contributing significantly to the legal equality of the sexes. Among the congressional (13) <u>initiatives</u> that have helped women are the Equal Pay Act of 1963, which (14) <u>prohibits</u> sex

(15) <u>discrimination</u> in salary and wages by some categories of employers; the Civil Rights Act of 1964, which prohibits sex discrimination in programs that receive federal funding; Title IX of the Education Amendment of 1972, which prohibits sex discrimination in education; the Equal Credit Act of 1974, as amended in 1976, which prohibits sex discrimination in the granting of financial credit; and the Civil Rights Act of 1991 and the Family Leave Act of 1993.

Women have made clear gains in the area of appointive and elective offices. In 1981 President Reagan appointed the first woman to serve on the Supreme Court, Sandra Day O'Connor. When the Democratic party in 1984 chose Geraldine Ferraro as its vice-presidential nominee, it was the first time a woman ran on the national ticket of a major political party. The elections of Ann Richards in Texas (1990) and Christine Todd Whitman in New Jersey (1993) marked another milestone: for the first time, two large states had a woman as the (16) <u>incumbent</u> governor. In 1992, Barbara Boxer and Dianne Feinstein were elected to the U.S. Senate from California, the first time that women have held both Senate seats in a state. Despite such signs of progress, women are still a long way from political equality with men. Women occupy about 10 percent of the nation's (17) <u>gubernatorial</u> and congressional offices, and women who hold lower public offices are more likely than their male counterparts to believe there are significant obstacles to political advancement.

However, the women's vote is becoming increasingly (18) <u>potent</u>. A few decades ago, there was (19) <u>virtually</u> no difference in the (20) <u>partisan</u> voting of men and women. Today, there is a pronounced "gender gap." It reached a record high in the 1994 congressional elections when women voted nearly 10 percent more Democratic than men. The gender gap is particularly pronounced when a woman is running on the Democratic ticket. When Senators Feinstein and Boxer won election in 1992, each scored 14 percentage points higher among women than men.

Exercise 1: Summary

Before you begin to zero in on the underlined words in the passage, try to talk with a fellow student about the content of the passage. Then, in your own words, write a brief summary of what you have learned about women's equality. Include some specific details about what guarantees that women will not face discrimination.

_____

_____

_____

_____

_____

Exercise 2: Example

Give an example of a situation in which a woman might face discrimination. Tell what recourse she might have to fight such discrimination.

_____

_____

_____

_____

_____

Exercise 3: Definitions

Working on your own or with a fellow student, try to define the underlined words from the selection you have just read. You will need to rely on the context and your own background knowledge for the definitions. Write each definition in the space provided after the word.

1. disregard

_____

2. essentially

_____

3. dispose

_____

4. consent

_____

5. violation

_____

6. barred

_____

7. aligned

_____

8. abolitionist

_____

9. abridged

_____

10. amendment

_____

11. ratification

_____

12. forefront

_____

13. initiatives

_____

14. prohibits

_____

15. discrimination

_____

16. incumbent

_____

17. gubernatorial

_____

18. potent

_____

19. virtually

_____

20. partisan

_____

Now compare your answers to the definitions in the word list that follows. Since your definitions are written in your own words, they will probably be less formal and more understandable for you. Check to be sure that the content is essentially the same, but don't substitute the dictionary-type definitions for your own. You will find that learning definitions in your own words rather than memorizing the ones in the book will help you learn the meanings better and remember them longer.

WORD LIST

The words listed below are the ones that you are studying in this chapter. Although you have met them in the context of a history passage, you may find some of them in other types of textbooks, newspapers, magazines, professional journals, and recreational reading sources as well.

1. **abolitionist** (ab ə lish′ ə nist), *n.* one who advocates doing away with slavery.

2. **abridge** (ə brij′), *v.* **1.** to deprive or cut off. **2.** to shorten, as *an abridged dictionary.* **3.** to diminish or curtail.

3. **align** (ə līn), *v.* **1.** to bring into agreement regarding a cause. **2.** to bring into line, as in *tire alignment.*

4. **amendment** (ə mend′ mənt), *n.* **1.** an addition or change to a bill, law, or the constitution. **2.** a modification or change.

5. **bar** (bär), *v.* **1.** to prevent or exclude. **2.** to fasten with a bar to confine or keep someone out. *n.* **3.** a long narrow piece of wood or metal. **4.** the railing in a law court. **5.** an oblong piece of material, as a *bar of soap or candy.* **6.** a strip of sand that appears above the surface of the water. **7.** a counter where drinks are served.

6. **consent** (kən sent′), *n.* **1.** permission or approval. **2.** agreement. *v.* **3.** to permit, approve, or comply.

7. **discrimination** (dis krim′ ə nā′ shən), *n.* **1.** policies or treatment based on prejudice. **2.** the process of making distinctions or differentiating.

8. **dispose** (of) (dis pōz′), *v.* **1.** to get rid of; settle; sell. (dispose) **2.** to be inclined or have a tendency, as in *disposed to accept.* **3.** to arrange.

9. **disregard** (dis ri gärd′), *n.* **1.** lack of attention or respect; neglect. **2.** to pay no attention to; to ignore.

10. **essentially** (ə sen′ shə lē), *adv.* **1.** by its very nature. **2.** having the greatest importance.

11. **forefront** (fôr′ frunt), *n.* **1.** the first place of importance. **2.** a position of prominence.

12. **gubernatorial** (goo′ bər nə tôr ē əl), *adj.* pertaining to the office of state governor.

13. **incumbent** (in kum′ bənt), *n.* **1.** the holder of an office. *adj.* **2.** obligatory, as a duty.

14. **initiative** (i nish′ ə tiv), *n.* **1.** an introductory step. **2.** self-reliance or readiness.

15. **partisan** (pär′ tə zen) *adj.* pertaining to a particular party, philosophy, or cause. *n.* **2.** a supporter of a person or party.

16. **potent** (pōt′ ənt), *adj.* **1.** powerful; mighty. **2.** chemically or medically effective. **3.** capable of sexual intercourse.

17. **prohibit** (prō hib′ it), *v.* **1.** to forbid by law or authority. **2.** to prevent from doing something.

18. **ratification** (rat ə fə kā′ shən), *n.* the act of approving, confirming, or accepting formally.

19. **violation** (vī ə lā′ shən), *n.* the act of infringement, a breach of law or promise.

20. **virtually** (vər′ chōo ə lē), *adv.* almost entirely; for the most part; just about all.

Exercise 4: Matching

Match the terms in column A with their definitions in column B.

	Column A	*Column B*
_____ 1.	align	a. approval or confirmation
_____ 2.	discrimination	b. for the most part
_____ 3.	disregard	c. first step
_____ 4.	gubernatorial	d. to move into agreement
_____ 5.	dispose (of)	e. shortened or curtailed
_____ 6.	virtually	f. show no respect
_____ 7.	violation	g. relating to the office of governor
_____ 8.	initiative	h. sell or eliminate
_____ 9.	ratification	i. breach of law or promise
_____ 10.	abridged	j. prejudiced treatment

	Column A	*Column B*
_____ 11.	prohibits	k. by its nature
_____ 12.	amendment	l. related to a party or cause

_____ 13.   consent   m. a primary position

_____ 14.   incumbent   n. powerful

_____ 15.   essentially   o. agreement or compliance

_____ 16.   potent   p. forbids or prevents

_____ 17.   barred   q. one holding office

_____ 18.   partisan   r. kept from; excluded

_____ 19.   abolitionist   s. one who advocates the
                                   elimination of slavery

_____ 20.   forefront   t. a change

Exercise 5: Fill-In

Choose the word that best completes each sentence below and write its letter in the space provided.

a. potent   d. forefront   g. violation   i. consent
b. essentially   e. initiative   h. abridged   j. prohibits
c. aligned   f. disregard

_____ 1. At the _____ of the women's movement was Betty
          Friedan who raised many issues with the publication of *The
          Feminine Mystique.*

_____ 2. The two horses finished at _____ the same time, so a

          photo was used to determine the winner.

_____ 3. When Charles built his garage, it was in _____ of the
          town ordinance that requires buildings to be 15 feet from the
          property line.

_____ 4. The English teacher would not allow her students to read an

          _____ version of *Great Expectations.*

_____ 5. The college policy _____ smoking inside any campus
          building.

_____ 6. On her own _____, Emily called the newspaper to
          cover the student protest meeting.

_____ 7. The investment broker was reprimanded and fined after he

          sold his client's stocks and bonds without her _____.

_____ 8. The customer was so offended by the _____ of the store clerks that she refused to shop there and encouraged her friends to stay away.

_____ 9. There was no clear majority candidate, so two of the parties _____ themselves behind a compromise candidate.

_____ 10. The defense attorney presented such a _____ argument that the jury returned a not-guilty verdict within two hours.

Exercise 6: Application

Title IX has had a significant influence on high school and college sports for girls and women. Based on what you know from your own experience, your reading, or what you can infer from the passage, tell what effect you think the law has had since it was passed in 1972.

_____

_____

_____

_____

_____

ART: CENSORSHIP

6

The issue of censorship is one that particularly affects artists, writers, and musicians. Because of the constitutional guarantees of freedom of expression and the need to be uninhibited in their work, artists usually resent outsiders telling them what is "unacceptable." On the other side of the argument are those who believe the public should not be exposed to pornographic or socially unacceptable material. One significant question is, Who decides what is socially acceptable and what is not? In the following passage, you will read about some guidelines that have been used to determine what is art. Even with guidelines, though, the issue is not an easy one, and interpretations often differ. Before you read the passage, think about your own position on censorship. Should artists be allowed to express themselves freely, or should the publication of their work be restricted if it is offensive? You may want to discuss this issue with your instructor and classmates. After you have read the passage, which includes examples of censorship cases, see if your opinion on the subject has changed.

Read the following passage about censorship to learn something about attempts to keep artists from exhibiting works considered obscene by others.

CENSORSHIP

Each of the arts has had its lightning rods—works that, because of their form or content, attract the storm of attention and passion and (1) <u>controversy</u>. These same works usually raise the issue of censorship. In literature it was D. H. Lawrence's *Lady Chatterley's Lover*, which, because of its (2) <u>explicit</u> sex scenes, was banned from publication in the United States for more than thirty years. In theater it was the musical *Hair*, which in 1968 confronted Broadway audiences with a shockingly new sight: the entire cast stark naked. And in photography it was the "X Portfolio" of Robert Mapplethorpe.

Starting in 1976, with his first (3) <u>solo</u> exhibition, Mapplethorpe gained considerable fame but the fame acquired a troublesome edge when the public at large became aware of his "X Portfolio." For that series of photographs contains images of (4) <u>sadomasochism</u> and (5) <u>homoeroticism</u>, images so frank as to be profoundly disturbing to many (even most) viewers.

Mapplethorpe died of AIDS in the spring of 1989. Soon after, an exhibition of his work was organized, including several examples from the "X Portfolio." The show was planned to tour the United States. Here the (6) <u>saga</u> begins, and it probably will be discussed and debated in art circles for many years to come.

The Mapplethorpe show was scheduled to open at Washington's Corcoran Gallery of Art, a public museum, in the summer of 1989. Before the opening, however, it came to the attention of Senator Jesse Helms, Republican of North Carolina, who (7) <u>denounced</u> the photographs as (8) <u>obscene</u>. Senator Helms' chief objection was that part of the funding for the exhibition had come from the National Endowment for the Arts—in other words, from American taxpayers. His attempt to persuade Congress to prohibit funding for work he considered obscene caused a (9) <u>furor</u>, with intense argument on both sides. In the heat of this controversy, the Corcoran canceled, but the show later opened, to general (10) <u>acclaim</u>, at Washington's Project for the Arts.

After Washington, the Mapplethorpe show moved to Hartford, Connecticut, and Berkeley, California; in both places it ran without major incident or protest. Next on the (11) <u>itinerary</u>, however, was a city well known for its strict opposition to (12) <u>pornography</u>: Cincinnati. And in

Cincinnati the controversy became an uproar. No longer was the issue merely public funding. Now it became: Should these photographs be shown at all?

On opening day in Cincinnati, police closed the Contemporary Arts Center while they videotaped the exhibition for evidence. Then the exhibition was reopened, and it played to huge crowds for the (13) <u>duration</u> of its stay. But a grand jury indicted both the gallery and its director on obscenity charges. If convicted, the gallery's director could serve up to a year in jail.

Before discussing the outcome of the trial, it might be well to pause and consider some of the issues involved. Is the Mapplethorpe case really a matter of censorship, and what, in fact, is censorship? For our purposes here, we will define (14) *censorship* as the supervision by one individual or group over the artistic expression of another individual or group. This definition assumes that person or group A has the power to *control* the expression of person or group B. Usually, the power is (15) <u>exerted</u> for political, religious, or moral reasons. In other words, A can prevent B from making or showing work that conflicts with A's political, religious, or moral point of view.

We expect to find censorship in (16) <u>totalitarian</u> societies, and we are seldom disappointed. Absolute rule survives only *because* it is absolute, so it cannot tolerate other points of view. But in the United States today censorship for political reasons is far less an issue than is censorship concerning religious or moral standards.

We have a (17) <u>pluralistic</u> society, representing many religions, many moral points of view. People of goodwill and thoughtful convictions disagree about what is "right" or "wrong," what should be allowed or not allowed. One of the most explosive areas of disagreement concerns the issue of free expression, specifically as it pertains to the arts. Should artists, writers, and performers be allowed to express whatever they wish? Or should there be limits on that expression to control material that large segments of society consider morally wrong?

Proponents of free expression cite the First Amendment to the Constitution, which states in part: "Congress shall make no law . . . abridging the freedom of speech." Yet that amendment does not give you the right to say anything you please. You cannot, for example, deliberately tell a lie about another person, either verbally (slander) or in print (libel). Such lies are prohibited, and the other person could sue you.

In a classic example from the early part of this century, Supreme Court Justice Oliver Wendell Holmes, Jr., said, "No one has a right falsely to shout 'fire' in a crowded theatre." So freedom of speech is not absolute; it has limits. Moreover, the Supreme Court historically has held that it is permissible to ban obscene speech, obscene writing, obscene imagery. The problem lies in deciding just *what* is obscene.

As of this writing the Supreme Court standard for obscenity comes from a 1973 case called *Miller v. California*, which held that something is obscene if the "average person applying contemporary community standards" would find it so, and if "the work taken as a whole lacks serious literary, artistic, political or scientific value." Obviously, this judgment raises more questions than it answers. Who is the average person? Which community? Who decides whether the artistic value is serious?

Further complicating the problem is the issue of public funding for the arts. Many people feel that taxpayers' money should not be used to support the arts at all. Others think the government should finance the arts, but not "obscene" art—whatever that is. Those who oppose limits on spending fear that such limits would lead to a situation like the one that has existed in totalitarian societies, where government controls the arts (18) <u>rigidly</u>.

In our system we pay our taxes and allow our elected representatives to decide how the money should be spent. And in 1965 Congress passed the National Foundation on the Arts and Humanities Act, whose declaration of purpose includes this statement: "It is necessary and appropriate for the Federal Government to help create and sustain not only a climate encouraging freedom of thought, imagination and inquiry, but also the material conditions (19) <u>facilitating</u> the release of this creative talent."

Again as of this writing, funding for the National Endowment for the Arts will continue, but the question of funding for "obscene" art—and the method of determining what is "obscene"—remains vague. Of course, there will *never* be absolute answers to any of these questions, answers acceptable to everyone. Readers of this book must make up their own minds, as the courts continue to grapple with these complex issues. And that brings us back to the Mapplethorpe case.

Six months after the Cincinnati gallery and its director were indicted on obscenity charges, a jury of local citizens found them not guilty. The jurors were not art experts; most of them had never been in an art museum, knew nothing about art, and cared little about it. Yet they were willing to be guided by the opinions of people who were presented to them as experts, art professionals brought in by the defense. As one juror said afterward, "We had to go with what we were told. It's like Picasso. Picasso from what everybody tells me was an artist. It's not my cup of tea. I don't understand it. But if people say it's art, then I have to go along with it." Another juror explained his decision this way: "We thought the pictures were lewd, grotesque, disgusting. But like the defense said, art doesn't have to be beautiful or pretty."

Mapplethorpe jurors were "average persons" who, even when applying the standards of a rather conservative "community," found that the works in question *did* have "serious artistic value." That was the (20) <u>resolution</u> of one case, but there will be many cases, and the question of censorship can never have a definite answer.

Exercise 1: Summary

Before you begin to zero in on the underlined words in the passage, try to talk with a fellow student about the content of the passage. Then, in your own words, write a brief summary of what you have learned about censorship. Include a definition of censorship and tell how you think it should be applied to artists.

_____

_____

_____

_____

_____

Exercise 2: Example

Give an example of a situation in which you think censorship might be justified. Tell why.

_____

_____

_____

_____

_____

Exercise 3: Definitions

Working on your own or with a fellow student, try to define the underlined words from the selection you have just read. In many cases, you can find the definition in the text. The notation "(stated)" or "(partially stated)" will tell you when this is so. For other terms, you will need to rely on the context and your own background knowledge. Write each definition in the space provided after the word.

1. controversy

   _____

2. explicit

   _____

3. solo

   _____

4. sadomasochism

   _____

5. homoeroticism

   _____

6. saga

   _____

7. denounced

   _____

8. obscene (partially stated)

   _____

9. furor

   _____

10. acclaim

    _____

11. itinerary

    _____

12. pornography

    _____

13. duration

    _____

14. censorship (stated)

    _____

15. exerted

    _____

16. totalitarian

_____

17. pluralistic

_____

18. rigidly

_____

19. facilitating

_____

20. resolution

_____

Now compare your answers to the definitions in the word list that follows. Since your definitions are written in your own words, they will probably be less formal and more understandable for you. Check to be sure that the content is essentially the same, but don't substitute the dictionary-type definitions for your own. You will find that learning definitions in your own words rather than memorizing the ones in the book will help you learn the meanings better and remember them longer.

WORD LIST

The words listed below are the ones that you are studying in this chapter. Although you have met them in the context of an art passage, you may find some of them in other types of textbooks, newspapers, magazines, professional journals, and recreational reading sources as well.

1. **acclaim** (ə klām′), _n._ **1.** approval or praise. _v._ **2.** to applaud or praise.
2. **censorship** (sen′ sər ship), _n._ the supervision by one individual or group over the artistic expression of another individual or group.
3. **controversy** (kon′ trə vər sē), _n._ a dispute; a differing of opinions.
4. **denounce** (di nouns′), _v._ **1.** to publicly accuse of blame. **2.** to condemn.
5. **duration** (doo rā′ shən), _n._ the length of time something lasts.
6. **exert** (ig zûrt′), _v._ to bring forth or put into action.
7. **explicit** (ik splis′ it), _adj._ expressed fully and precisely.
8. **facilitate** (fə sil′ ə tāt), _v._ to make easier; to assist someone's progress.

9. **furor** (fyoor′ ər), *n.* **1.** an uproar. **2.** contagious excitement. **3.** anger.

10. **homoeroticism** (hō′ mō i rot′ ə siz əm), *n.* sexual arousal in response to a member of the same sex.

11. **itinerary** (ī tin′ ə rer ē), *n.* a plan or route for a journey or trip.

12. **obscene** (əb sēn′), *adj.* **1.** repulsive or offensive. **2.** describing a work that lacks serious literary, artistic, political, or scientific value.

13. **pluralistic** (ploor′ ə lis tik), *adj.* characteristic of a society where minority groups participate and have their differences respected.

14. **pornography** (pôr nog′ rə fē), *n.* writings, pictures, or movies designed to cause sexual excitement and having little artistic merit.

15. **resolution** (rez ə loo′ shən), *n.* **1.** a solution or settlement of a controversy. **2.** a formal statement of opinion. **3.** the process of solving or determining a course of action.

16. **rigid** (rij′ id), *adj.* **1.** strict or unyielding. **2.** stiff or inflexible.

17. **sadomasochism** (sā′ dō mas′ ə kiz əm), *n.* sexual gratification through inflicting or receiving pain.

18. **saga** (sä′ gə), *n.* **1.** a story or tale. **2.** a legend or epic of heroic deeds.

19. **solo** (sō′ lō), *adj.* **1.** pertaining to being or performing on one's own. *n.* **2.** a performance by one person.

20. **totalitarian** (tō ta lə ter′ ē ən), *adj.* relating to a government that exercises strict controls and does not tolerate differences of opinion.

Exercise 4: Matching

Match the terms in column A with their definitions in column B.

	Column A	Column B
_____ 1.	exert	a. trip plan or route
_____ 2.	solo	b. applause or praise
_____ 3.	itinerary	c. sexual arousal in response to a member of one's own sex
_____ 4.	duration	d. to put forth
_____ 5.	pluralistic	e. public dispute
_____ 6.	facilitate	f. to publicly criticize or condemn

_____	7.	denounce	g. on one's own
_____	8.	homoeroticism	h. describing a varied society
_____	9.	controversy	i. length of time
_____	10.	acclaim	j. to ease or assist

	Column A	*Column B*
_____ 11.	furor	k. supervision of someone's else's artistic expression
_____ 12.	saga	l. solution
_____ 13.	resolution	m. sexually exciting without artistic value
_____ 14.	totalitarian	n. strict
_____ 15.	censorship	o. an uproar
_____ 16.	pornography	p. offensive or repulsive
_____ 17.	explicit	q. sexual gratification through pain
_____ 18.	sadomasochism	r. governing with little freedom
_____ 19.	obscene	s. lengthy story
_____ 20.	rigid	t. clear and fully expressed

Exercise 5: Fill-In

Choose the word that best completes each sentence below and write its letter in the space provided.

a. pluralistic	d. denounce	g. obscene	i. facilitate
b. totalitarian	e. itinerary	h. exert	j. resolution
c. controversy	f. duration		

_____ 1. Having grown up in a _____ society, Anatoly remained reluctant to express his opinions even after living in the United States for five years.

_____ 2. School administrators and parents are concerned that children may be exposed to _____ material on the Internet.

_____ 3. For the _____ of her stay in New York City, Jolanda decided to rely on public transportation as a way to cut down on her expenses.

_____ 4. The English teacher had no idea that assigning a book like *Manchild in the Promised Land* would cause such a

_____.

_____ 5. The judge was pleased to learn that the neighbors had

reached a _____ to their dispute before the case came to trial.

_____ 6. When Anand left on his three-week business trip, he left his

_____ with his secretary so he could contact him in an emergency.

_____ 7. Children who grow up on the east or west coast of the

United States often experience a _____ society partially due to the arrival of many immigrants.

_____ 8. Once Laura reached eighteen, her parents seemed to have

lost their power to _____ their influence over her choice of friends.

_____ 9. To _____ the registration process, counselors and academic advisers were available all week for student conferences.

_____ 10. Even though she is personally opposed to abortion, Ruth

refused to _____ women who chose to have one.

Exercise 6: Application

Pretend that you are in charge of an exhibition of student work. Students will submit drawings, paintings, and photographs for an exhibit that will be on display in the school library. What instructions would you give your selection committee to determine which works to display? How should they handle controversial works? Defend your position.

_____

_____

_____

_____

_____

MUSIC:
MUSICAL
INSTRUMENTS

7

Music is a topic with which most people are familiar and which they are usually willing to discuss. Personal tastes in music are often quite definite. A frequent comment is, "I know what I like when I hear it." Most people who are not serious students of music don't really understand what distinguishes one type of music from another. The passage in this chapter is a basic introduction to types of musical instruments. In an introductory music class, this is a topic that would probably be covered at the beginning of the semester. The vocabulary words in this chapter represent a combination of general words that you would find in any passage and technical words associated with the field of music. What a music professor would expect from his or her students after studying this chapter is a knowledge of the types of musical instruments and how they differ according to category.

Read the following passage about the types of musical instruments to be able to identify and describe them.

MUSICAL INSTRUMENTS

People around the world use musical instruments that vary greatly in construction and tone color. An (1) *instrument* may be defined as any mechanism—other than the voice—that produces musical sounds. Western musicians usually classify instruments in six broad categories: (2)*string* (such as guitar and violin); (3) *woodwind* (flute, clarinet); (4) *brass* (trumpet, trombone); (5) *percussion* (bass drum, cymbals); (6) *keyboard* (organ, piano); and *electronic* (synthesizer).[1]

An instrument is often made in different sizes that produce different ranges. For instance, the saxophone family includes soprano, alto, tenor, baritone, and bass saxophones.

An instrument's tone color may vary with the (8) *register* (part of the total range) in which it is played. A clarinet sounds dark and rich in its low register, but its high register is brilliant and piercing.

Instrumental performers try to match the beautiful (9) flexible tone of a singer's voice. Yet most instruments have a wider range of pitches than the voice does. While a trained singer's range is about 2 (10) octaves, many instruments command 3 or 4 octaves, and some have 6 or 7. Also, instruments usually produce tones more rapidly than the voice. When writing music for a specific instrument, composers have to consider its range of pitches and (11) dynamics and how fast it can produce (12) tones.

Instruments provide entertainment and accompany singing, dancing, religious (13) rites, and drama. But they have served other functions, too. In some cultures, instruments are thought to have magic

[1]The scientific classification of instruments, based on the way sound is made, has five categories: *chordophones* (a stretched string is the sound generator—our "string" category); *aerophones* (a column of air is the sound generator—our "woodwind" and "brass" categories); *ideophones* (instruments whose own material is the sound generator, such as cymbals, gongs, and bells—part of our "percussion" category); *membranophones* (instruments with a stretched skin or other membrane as the sound generator, such as drums—part of our "percussion" category); and *electrophones* (instruments generating their sounds by means of electricity—our "electronic" category).

powers. Bells are worn to guard against harm, and rattlers are used by traditional healers. In parts of Africa, drums are so sacred that religious rites are not performed without them, and special ceremonies and sacrifices are sometimes (14) <u>enacted</u> when the drums are being made.

Instruments have been used for communication as well. Detailed messages have been sent by drumbeats; hunters have blown horns for signals, and musicians have announced the time by sounding brass instruments from towers. Trumpets have been used for military signals and to (15) <u>bolster</u> soldiers' courage in battle. For centuries, trumpets and kettledrums announced kings and queens.

Musical instruments have even been status symbols. During the nineteenth and early twentieth centuries, the piano was a fixture in any home that (16) <u>aspired</u> to be middle-class. "Proper" young ladies were expected to learn the piano as one of many "accomplishments." Such ideas lost their (17) <u>currency</u> when women began to move more freely in the world (around the time of World War I), and when the radio and phonograph began to replace the piano as a source of home entertainment. Still, even today there are status (18) <u>implications</u> in the type of audio equipment someone owns. Though a stereo is not a musical instrument, a connection can be made between the parlor piano of 1900 and today's elaborate "home entertainment centers."

Instruments' popularity rises and falls with changing musical tastes and requirements. Today only a fraction of all known instruments are used. However, interest in music of earlier times has led to the (19) <u>resurrection</u> of instruments like the harpsichord, an ancestor of the piano; and the recorder, a relative of the flute. Modern (20) <u>replicas</u> of ancient instruments are being built and played. In fact, modern musicians are flexible and far-ranging in their choice of instruments. Rock composers have used nonwestern instruments such as the Indian sitar (a plucked string instrument). Jazz musicians are turning to classical instruments like the flute, while classical composers are using instruments associated with jazz, such as the vibraphone.

Compositions may be written for solo instruments, for small groups, and for orchestras with over 100 musicians. Whatever the group, it may include instruments from only one category (say, strings) or from several categories. Modern symphony orchestras contain string, woodwind, brass, and percussion instruments. Keyboard instruments also find their way into the modern orchestra as needed. Bands consist mainly of brass, woodwind, and percussion instruments.

Exercise 1: Summary

Before you begin to zero in on the underlined words in the passage, try to talk with a fellow student about the content of the passage. Then, in your own words, write a brief summary of what you have learned about musical instruments. Include a list of the six classifications of instruments.

_____

_____

_____

_____

_____

Exercise 2: Examples

Give two examples of the purposes for which musical instruments are used.

_____

_____

_____

_____

_____

Exercise 3: Definitions

Working on your own or with a fellow student, try to define the underlined words from the selection you have just read. In many cases, you can find the definition in the text. The notation "(stated)" will tell you when this is so. For other terms, you will need to rely on the context and your own background knowledge. Write each definition in the space provided after the word.

1. instrument (stated)

   _____

2. string (instrument)

   _____

3. woodwind (instrument)

   _____

4. brass (instrument)

_____

5. percussion (instrument)

_____

6. keyboard (instrument)

_____

7. electronic (instrument)

_____

8. register (stated)

_____

9. flexible

_____

10. octaves

_____

11. dynamics

_____

12. tones

_____

13. rites

_____

14. enacted

_____

15. bolster

_____

16. aspired

_____

17. currency

_____

18. implications

_____

19. resurrection

_____

20. replicas

_____

Now compare your answers to the definitions in the word list that follows. Since your definitions are written in your own words, they will probably be less formal and more understandable for you. Check to be sure that the content is essentially the same, but don't substitute the dictionary-type definitions for your own. You will find that learning definitions in your own words rather than memorizing the ones in the book will help you learn the meanings better and remember them longer.

WORD LIST

The words listed below are the ones that you are studying in this chapter. Although you have met them in the context of a music passage, you may find some of them in other types of textbooks, newspapers, magazines, professional journals, and recreational reading sources as well.

1. **aspire** (ə spīr'), _v._ to aim or seek to accomplish something, like a goal.

2. **bolster** (bōl' stər), _v._ **1.** to support or boost. _n._ **2.** a long, tubular-shaped pillow.

3. **brass** (instrument) (bras), _n._ a musical wind instrument of brass or other metal with a cup-shaped mouthpiece, as a trumpet or trombone.

4. **currency** (kər' ən sē), _n._ **1.** general use or wide acceptance. **2.** a form of money in circulation.

5. **dynamics** (dī nam' iks), _n._ **1.** variation in the volume of musical sound. **2.** the study of physical forces and motion. **3.** the driving forces in a field or system.

6. **electronic** (instrument) (i lek tron' ik), _n._ a musical instrument that uses electronics to produce or amplify the sound.

7. **enact** (in akt'), _v._ **1.** to act out, as in a play. **2.** to make into law.

8. **flexible** (flek' sə bəl), _adj._ **1.** readily changed; capable of adaptation. **2.** easily bent; pliable.

9. **implication** (im pli kā' shən), _n._ a consequence which is suggested or understood.

10. **instrument** (in' strə ment), _n._ any mechanism that produces musical sounds.

11. **keyboard** (instrument) (kē′ bôrd), *n.* a musical instrument played with a pianolike set of keys, as an organ.

12. **octave** (ok′ tiv), *n.* **1.** a musical interval including eight degrees. **2.** a musical tone on the eighth degree from a given tone. **3.** a series of tones extending through an interval.

13. **percussion** (instrument) (pər kush′ ən), *n.* an instrument that produces sound by beating, striking, or shaking.

14. **register** (rej′ ə stər), *n.* **1.** the range of a voice or an instrument. **2.** a book of records. **3.** a device to control heating ventilation. **4.** an automatic device for recording data, as a cash register.

15. **replica** (rep′ li kə), *n.* a copy or reproduction.

16. **resurrection** (rez ə rek′ shən), *n.* **1.** a revival or bringing back to life. **2.** the act of rising from the dead.

17. **rite** (rīt), *n.* a formal ceremony or religious practice.

18. **string** (instrument) (string), *n.* an instrument in which the sound is produced by a string, often played with a bow, as a violin.

19. **tones** (tōnz), *n.* sounds of definite pitch.

20. **woodwind** (instrument) (wood′ wind), *n.* an instrument that uses a column of air to produce sound, as a flute, clarinet, oboe, or bassoon.

Exercise 4: Matching

Match the terms in column A with their definitions in column B.

		Column A	*Column B*
_____	1.	rite	a. a mechanism that produces musical sounds
_____	2.	bolster	b. revival
_____	3.	currency	c. adaptable
_____	4.	woodwind	d. religious ceremony
_____	5.	instrument	e. an instrument that produces sound electronically
_____	6.	dynamics	f. an instrument that produces sound by beating
_____	7.	flexible	g. wide acceptability

_____ 8. electronic   h. an instrument that produces sound through a column of air

_____ 9. percussion   i. to provide support

_____ 10. resurrection   j. variation on volume

Column A	*Column B*

_____ 11. aspire   k. a reproduction

_____ 12. string   l. to portray or act out

_____ 13. implication   m. an instrument that produces sound with pianolike keys

_____ 14. tone   n. something suggested

_____ 15. replica   o. a musical instrument made of metal

_____ 16. enact   p. a musical interval

_____ 17. octave   q. a musical sound of definite pitch

_____ 18. register   r. a musical instrument played with a bow

_____ 19. brass   s. the range of an instrument

_____ 20. keyboard   t. to strive toward a goal

Exercise 5: Fill-In

Choose the word that best completes each sentence below and write its letter in the space provided.

a. bolster   d. currency   g. tone   i. flexible
b. aspire   e. replica   h. instrument   j. resurrection
c. implication   f. rites

_____ 1. Lisa did not realize the _____ of cheating on the test until she was called to appear before the academic standards committee.

_____ 2. Saul's guidance counselor encouraged him to _____ to be an accountant rather than a bookkeeper because of his thinking skills.

_____ 3. At the beginning of fourth grade, each child was given an opportunity to learn to play an _____.

_____ 4. At the Easter service, the _____ of the solo was clear and beautiful.

_____ 5. Maurice is a _____ musician, able to play in the school orchestra as well as with his rock group.

_____ 6. The young violinist's teacher tried to _____ his confidence before he walked onto the stage.

_____ 7. To increase subscriptions, the concert series' director had to update the _____ of the performances.

_____ 8. Danisha was delighted with the _____ of the hammered dulcimer, built to look like one used in the Middle Ages.

_____ 9. After being baptized and confirmed, Donnell was able to participate fully in the _____ of his church.

_____ 10. The _____ of the jazz band at the high school occurred after a graduate and former member returned as the music director

Exercise 6: Application

Explain to a child who is choosing an instrument to learn to play what categories are available. Recommend one type of instrument and tell why you would choose it.

_____

_____

_____

_____

PSYCHOLOGY:
CLASSICAL
CONDITIONING

8

In this chapter you will learn a bit about the field of psychology and some vocabulary words that will help you to understand it. First you will read an adapted excerpt from a first-year psychology textbook. Some of the terms in the reading will be numbered and underlined. Your first task will be to define them either from context or from the stated definition. In the following exercises, you will practice using the terms.

Psychology is a field dedicated to the study of human behavior. The word itself comes from two word parts: the root *psyche* meaning mind and the suffix *ology* meaning the study of. Many college students enroll in an introductory psychology course in their first or second semesters. In some cases, it helps them decide to pursue a major in the social sciences. In other cases, the course satisfies a social science requirement for students whose major area of study is another field. Many first-time psychology students are fascinated by the possibilities of analyzing and predicting their own behavior and others' on the basis of psychological study. As with many fields, psychology has a language of its own. Students who master the terminology will have an easier time grasping the concepts. As you study the words and phrases in this chapter, you will have a glimpse of the kinds of terms you will need to know if you study psychology. You will also gain some experience of how they are introduced in a textbook. Most psychology textbooks contain a glossary at the back of the book that includes definitions of words used in the text. In this chapter, most definitions are taken from the glossary. When you are using a textbook, take advantage of this resource. The glossary will provide you with the most appropriate definition for the word as it is used in the text. It may also refer you to specific page numbers where you can learn more about the word in context.

Read the following selection to learn about one area of psychology and an interesting experiment that demonstrates some of its findings.

CLASSICAL CONDITIONING

- *What is learning?*
- *How do we learn to form associations between stimuli and responses?*

Does the mere sight of the golden arches in front of McDonald's make you feel pangs of hunger and think about hamburgers? If it does, then you are displaying a (1) <u>rudimentary</u> form of learning called classical conditioning.

The processes that underlie classical conditioning explain such diverse phenomena as crying at the sight of a bride walking down the aisle at a wedding, fearing the dark, and falling in love with the boy or girl next door. To understand classical conditioning, however, it is necessary to move back in time and place to the early part of this century in Russia.

The Basics of Conditioning

Ivan Pavlov, a Russian (2) <u>physiologist</u>, never intended to do psychological research. In 1904 he won the Nobel Prize for his work on digestion, testimony to his contribution to that field. Yet Pavlov is remembered not for his physiological research, but for his experiments on basic learning processes—work that he began quite accidentally.

Pavlov had been studying the (3) <u>secretion</u> of stomach acids and (4) <u>salivation</u> in dogs in response to the ingestion of varying amounts and kinds of food. While doing so, he observed a curious phenomenon: Sometimes stomach-secretions and salivation would begin when no food had actually been eaten. The mere sight of a food bowl, the individual who normally brought the food, or even the sound of that individual's footsteps was enough to produce a physiological response in the dogs. Pavlov's genius was his ability to recognize the implications of this rather basic discovery. He saw that the dogs were responding not only on the basis of a biological need (hunger), but also as a result of learning—or, as it came to be called, classical conditioning. In (5) **classical conditioning**,[1] an organism learns to respond to a neutral stimulus that normally does not bring about that response.

[1]**Classical conditioning:** A kind of learning in which a previously neutral stimulus comes to elicit a response through its association with a stimulus that naturally brings about the response.

To demonstrate and analyze classical conditioning, Pavlov conducted a series of experiments. . . . In one, he attached a tube to the salivary gland of a dog, which allowed Pavlov to measure precisely the amount of salivation that occurred. He then sounded a tuning fork and, just a few seconds later, presented the dog with meat powder. This pairing, carefully planned so that exactly the same amount of time elapsed between the presentation of the sound and the meat powder, occurred repeatedly. At first the dog would salivate only when the meat powder itself was presented, but soon it began to salivate at the sound of the tuning fork. In fact, even when Pavlov stopped presenting the meat powder, the dog still salivated after hearing the sound. The dog had been classically conditioned to salivate to the tone.

As you can see in Figure 6-1, the basic processes of classical conditioning underlying Pavlov's discovery are straightforward, although the terminology he chose has a technical ring. Consider first the diagram in Figure 6-1a. Prior to conditioning, there are two unrelated stimuli: the sound of a tuning fork and meat powder. We know that the sound of a tuning fork leads not to salivation but to some irrelevant response such as perking of the ears or, perhaps, a startle reaction. The sound in this case is therefore called the (6) **neutral stimulus**[2] because it has no effect on the response of interest. We also have meat powder, which, because of the biological makeup of the dog, naturally leads to salivation, the response that we are interested in conditioning. The meat powder is considered an (7) **unconditioned stimulus, or UCS**[3] because food placed in a dog's mouth automatically causes salivation to occur. The response that the meat powder (8) elicits (salivation) is called an (9) **unconditioned response, or UCR**[4]—a response that is not associated with previous learning. Unconditioned responses are natural, innate responses that involve no training. They are always brought about by the presence of unconditioned stimuli.

Figure 6-1b illustrates what happens during conditioning. The tuning fork is repeatedly sounded just before presentation of the meat powder. The goal of conditioning is for the tuning fork to become associated with the unconditioned stimulus (meat powder) and therefore to bring about the same sort of response as the unconditioned stimulus. During this period, salivation gradually increases each time the tuning fork is sounded, until the tuning fork alone causes the dog to salivate.

[2]**Neutral stimulus:** A stimulus that, before conditioning, has no effect on the desired response.

[3]**Unconditioned stimulus (UCS):** A stimulus that brings about a response without having been learned.

[4]**Unconditioned response (UCR):** A response that is natural and needs no training (e.g., salivation at the smell of food.)

Figure 6–1

The basic process of classical conditioning. (*a*) Prior to conditioning, the sound of a tuning fork does not bring about salivation—making the tuning fork a neutral stimulus. On the other hand, meat powder naturally brings about salivation, making the meat powder an unconditioned stimulus and salivation an unconditioned response. (*b*) During conditioning, the tuning fork is sounded just before the presentation of the meat powder. (*c*) Eventually, the sound of the tuning fork alone brings about salivation. We can now say that conditioning has been accomplished: The previously neutral stimulus of the tuning fork is now considered a conditioned stimulus that brings about the conditioned response of salivation.

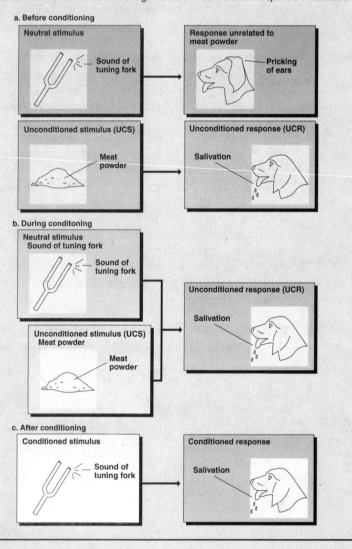

When conditioning is complete, the tuning fork has evolved from a neutral stimulus to what is now called a (10) **conditioned stimulus, or CS**.[5] At this time, salivation that occurs as a response to the conditioned stimulus (tuning fork) is considered a (11) **conditioned response, or CR**.[6] This situation is depicted in Figure 6-1c. After conditioning, then, the conditioned stimulus evokes the conditioned response.

The (12) <u>sequence</u> and timing of the presentation of the unconditioned stimulus and the conditioned stimulus are particularly important. . . . Like a malfunctioning railroad warning light at a street crossing that does not go on until after a train has passed by, a neutral stimulus that follows an unconditioned stimulus has little chance of becoming a conditioned stimulus. On the other hand, just as a warning light works best if it goes on right before a train is about to go by, a neutral stimulus that is presented just before the unconditioned stimulus is most apt to result in successful conditioning. Research has shown that conditioning is most effective if the neutral stimulus (which will become a conditioned stimulus) (13) <u>precedes</u> the unconditioned stimulus by between a half second and several seconds, depending on what kind of response is being conditioned.

Although the terminology employed by Pavlov to describe classical conditioning may at first seem confusing, the following rules of thumb can help to make the relationships between stimuli and responses easier to understand and *remember:*

- *Un*conditioned stimuli lead to *un*conditioned responses.

- *Un*conditioned stimulus–*un*conditioned response pairings are *un*-learned and *un*trained.

- During conditioning, previously neutral stimuli are transformed into conditioned stimuli.

- Conditioned stimuli lead to conditioned responses, and conditioned stimulus–conditioned response pairings are a consequence of learning and training.

- Unconditioned responses and conditioned responses are similar (such as salivation in the example described above), but the conditioned response is learned, whereas the unconditioned response occurs naturally.

[5]**Conditioned stimulus (CS):** A once-neutral stimulus that has been paired with an unconditioned stimulus to bring about a response formerly caused only by the unconditioned stimulus.

[6]**Conditioned response (CR):** A response that, after conditioning, follows a previously neutral stimulus (e.g., salivation at the sound of a tuning fork).

Applying Conditioning Principles to Human Behavior

Although the (14) <u>initial</u> experiments were carried out with animals, classical conditioning principles were soon found to explain many aspects of everyday human behavior. Recall, for instance, the earlier illustration of how people may experience hunger (15) <u>pangs</u> at the sight of McDonald's golden arches. The cause of this reaction is classical conditioning: The previously neutral arches have come to be associated with the food inside the restaurant (the unconditioned stimulus), causing the arches to become a conditioned stimulus that brings about the conditioned response of hunger.

Emotional responses are particularly likely to be learned through classical conditioning processes. For instance, how do some of us develop fears of mice, spiders, and other creatures that are typically harmless? In a now-famous case study designed to show that classical conditioning was at the root of such fears, an 11-month-old infant named Albert, who initially showed no fear of rats, heard a loud noise just as he was shown a rat. . . . The noise (the UCS) (16) <u>evoked</u> fear (the UCR). After just a few pairings of noise and rat, Albert began to show fear of the rat by itself. The rat, then, had become a CS that brought about the CR, fear. Similarly, the pairing of the appearance of certain species (such as mice or spiders) with the fearful comments of an adult may cause children to develop the same fears their parents have. [By the way, we don't know what happened to the unfortunate Albert. Watson, the experimenter, has been (17) <u>condemned</u> for using (18) <u>ethically</u> questionable procedures.]

In adulthood, learning via classical conditioning occurs a bit more (19) <u>subtly</u>. You may come to know that a job supervisor is in a bad mood when her tone of voice changes, if in the past you have heard her use that tone only when she was about to criticize someone's work. Likewise, you may not go to a dentist as often as you should because of (20) <u>prior</u> associations with dentists and pain. Or you may have a particular fondness for the color blue because that was the color of your childhood bedroom. Classical conditioning, then, explains many of the reactions we have to stimuli in the world around us. . . .

Exercise 1: Summary

Before you begin to zero in on the underlined words in the passage, try to talk with a fellow student about the content of the passage. Then, in your own words, write a brief summary of what you have learned about classical conditioning. Include some specific details about how the dog became "conditioned."

_____

_____

_____

_____

_____

Exercise 2: Example

Describe a situation you experienced or observed in which you, someone else, or an animal became "conditioned" to react in a particular way to a stimulus.

_____

_____

_____

_____

_____

Exercise 3: Definitions

Working on your own or with a fellow student, try to define the underlined words from the selection you have just read. In many cases, you can find the definition in the text. The notation "(stated)" will tell you when this is so. For other terms, you will need to rely on the context and your own background knowledge. Write each definition in the space provided after the word.

1. rudimentary

_____

2. physiologist

_____

3. secretion

_____

4. salivation

_____

5. classical conditioning (stated)

_____

6. neutral stimulus (stated)

_____

7. unconditioned stimulus (stated)

_____

8. elicits

_____

9. unconditioned response (stated)

_____

10. conditioned stimulus (stated)

_____

11. conditioned response (stated)

_____

12. sequence

_____

13. precedes

_____

14. initial

_____

15. pangs

_____

16. evoked

_____

17. condemned

_____

18. ethically

_____

19. subtly

_____

20. prior

_____

Now compare your answers to the definitions in the word list that follows. Since your definitions are written in your own words, they will probably be less formal and more understandable for you. Check to be sure that the content is essentially the same, but don't substitute the dictionary-type definitions for your own. You will find that learning definitions in your own words rather than memorizing the ones in the book will help you learn the meanings better and remember them longer.

WORD LIST

The words listed below are the ones that you are studying in this chapter. Although you have met them in the context of a psychology passage, you may find some of them in other types of textbooks, newspapers, magazines, professional journals, and recreational reading sources as well.

1. **classical conditioning** (klas′ i kəl kən dish′ ə ning) a process in which an organism learns to respond to a neutral stimulus that normally does not bring about that response.

2. **condemn** (kən dem′), v. **1.** to express strong disapproval. **2.** to convict of guilt. **3.** to sentence to punishment.

3. **conditioned response** (kən dish′ end ri spons′) a response that, after conditioning, follows a previously neutral stimulus.

4. **conditioned stimulus** (kən dish′ end stim′ yə ləs) a once-neutral stimulus that has been paired with an unconditioned stimulus to bring about a response formerly caused only by the unconditioned stimulus.

5. **elicit** (i lis′ it), v. to draw out or bring forth.

6. **ethical** (eth′ i kəl), adj. conforming to rules and standards for right or moral conduct.

7. **evoke** (i vōk′), v. to call forth or produce.

8. **initial** (i nish′ əl), adj. **1.** first, occurring at the beginning. n. **2.** the first letter of a name or word. v. **3.** to sign one's initials on a document.

9. **neutral stimulus** (nōō′ trəl stim′ yə les) a stimulus that, before conditioning, has no effect on the desired response.

10. **pang** (pang), n. a sudden, brief pain or feeling of physical or emotional distress.

11. **physiologist** (fiz ē ol′ ə jist), n. one who studies the branch of biology that deals with the functions of living organisms.

12. **precede** (pri sēd), v. to come or go before.

13. **prior** (prī′ ər), *adj.* earlier in time or order.

14. **rudimentary** (ro͞o də men′ tə rē), *adj.* elementary; basic; pertaining to first principles.

15. **salivation** (sal ə vā′ shən), *n.* the process of producing saliva, a watery solution secreted into the mouth that aids digestion.

16. **secretion** (si krē shən), *n.* **1.** the process of giving off a substance (in a cell or gland). **2.** the product of glandular activity.

17. **sequence** (sē′ kwens), *n.* chronological order of events.

18. **subtle** (sut′ əl), *adj.* **1.** hardly noticeable. **2.** fine or delicate. 3. difficult to perceive. 4. clever or sly.

19. **unconditioned response** a response that is natural and needs no training (e.g., salivation at the smell of food).

20. **unconditioned stimulus** a stimulus that brings about a response without having been learned.

Exercise 4: Matching

Match the terms in column A with their definitions in column B.

		Column A	Column B
_____	1.	unconditioned stimulus	a. comes before
_____	2.	classical conditioning	b. elementary; basic
_____	3.	evoke	c. glandular substance
_____	4.	pangs	d. something that brings about an unlearned reaction
_____	5.	rudimentary	e. a reaction to a previously neutral stimulus produced after conditioning
_____	6.	secretion	f. a type of learning that elicits a response after a neutral and natural stimulus have been paired
_____	7.	conditioned response	g. brief feelings of distress

_____ 8.   condemn   h. to call forth; bring out

_____ 9.   unconditioned   i. to strongly criticize
            response

_____ 10.   precedes   j. something that brings about
                                               an unlearned response

                        Column A   *Column B*

_____ 11.   ethical   k. understated

_____ 12.   initial   l. one who studies the functions
                                               of living things

_____ 13.   physiologist   m. something that has no effect
                                               on the desired response

_____ 14.   neutral stimulus   n. the act of producing a watery
                                               fluid in the mouth

_____ 15.   conditioned   o. beginning; first
            stimulus

_____ 16.   elicit   p. previous

_____ 17.   salivation   q. morally right or correct

_____ 18.   sequence   r. a once-neutral stimulus that
                                               now brings about a response

_____ 19.   subtle   s. an ordered or chronological
                                               arrangement

_____ 20.   prior   t. to bring out; produce

Exercise 5: Fill-In

Choose the word that best completes each sentence below and write its letter
in the space provided.

a. initial   d. physiologist   g. sequence   i. subtle
b. ethical   e. rudimentary   h. precede   j. condemn
c. prior   f. evoke

_____ 1. The doctor who helped a terminally ill patient commit

         suicide believed her behavior was _____ even if it was
         not yet legal.

_____ 2. After living in Mexico for two years, Jenn enrolled in

Spanish III without going through the required _____ of Spanish I and II.

_____ 3. When Calbert arrived in the United States for college, his

lack of knowledge of the _____ principles of algebra caused him great difficulty.

_____ 4. Yuri's _____ impression of his chemistry professor as rigid and unapproachable was disproved when he visited her during her office hours.

_____ 5. During acting class, the coach tried to _____ emotions of deep sadness from his students by asking them to focus on unhappy events.

_____ 6. Stephanie was ineligible to purchase additional insurance

because of a _____ medical condition that required frequent treatment.

_____ 7. In her sermon, the minister urged her parishioners to sympathize and support members of the congregation who

had sinned rather than to _____ them.

_____ 8. In her search for a position as a _____, Marina hoped to find one in a teaching hospital with a modern research laboratory.

_____ 9. On his first visit to the tattoo parlor, Alex learned that a

notarized permission slip from a parent must _____ any appointment to tattoo a minor.

_____ 10. Sheila searched for a perfume with a _____ aroma that would be more of a natural scent than an overwhelming one.

Exercise 6: Application

In addition to requiring their classes to learn the meanings of terms associated with a particular field, most professors also expect their students to be able to apply their knowledge to new situations. Once you have mastered the vocabulary of classical conditioning, you should be able to find examples of the concepts and use the correct terms in identifying them. In this exercise, you will be asked to identify the elements of classical conditioning you recognize.

A nursing mother consistently responds to her baby's crying by putting her baby to her breast. The baby's sucking causes the release of milk. Within a few days, as soon as the mother hears the baby crying, the milk starts to flow, even before she puts the baby to her breast.

1. What is the conditioned stimulus?

    _____

2. What is the conditioned response?

    _____

3. What is the unconditioned stimulus?

    _____

4. What is the unconditioned response?

    _____

MATH:
VARIABLES AND
ALGEBRAIC
EXPRESSIONS

9

College students can usually be categorized as math enthusiasts or math avoiders. Unfortunately, in college algebra classes, the avoiders often outnumber the enthusiasts. Algebra teachers report a high level of math anxiety among their students and frequent difficulty with word problems. Successful students must realize that effective reading strategies are essential to figuring out math word problems, and familiarity with the language of math is also critical. If you can succeed in these two areas, you are well on your way to becoming an excellent math student.

You will notice that the math passage is quite a bit shorter than the other passages in this book. The language of mathematics tends to be denser and more specific than that of other fields. It requires careful reading and close attention to terminology. Authors of math textbooks often include examples and sample problems to help you understand the concepts. Reviewing these is very important. Reading some explanatory paragraphs aloud and trying to provide some examples of your own also helps.

In the following passage, you will notice that many terms are printed in **boldface type.** Many authors use this type as a signal to the reader. In some cases, it indicates a heading or an important topic. In this passage, it identifies a new term that is usually followed by a definition. Math textbooks often introduce several new terms at the beginning of a chapter or section. Diagrams or figures may be included to help students visualize the terms. Definitions of the terms and problems that require students to apply the terms usually follow. Many students find that the application helps them to understand the definitions. The **boldface** terms in the following passage are those identified by the math textbook authors as important for understanding the material. The terms that are numbered and underlined, but printed in regular type, are words that are important but not necessarily math related. You can expect to meet them in other contexts as well.

The following passage appears in the first chapter of a college algebra book, and its purpose is to introduce some basic concepts and the language that goes with them.

Read the following selection about variables and algebraic expressions to learn how the language of algebra is used to convey information.

Barnett, Raymond and Kearns, Thomas J. From *Algebra for College Students* by Raymond A. Barnett and Thomas J. Kearns. Copyright © 1995 by The McGraw-Hill Companies. Reprinted with permission of The McGraw-Hill Companies.

VARIABLES AND ALGEBRAIC EXPRESSIONS

The letter x used in (1) <u>equations</u> such as $x^2 = 25$ is a variable. In general, a (2) **variable** is a symbol used to represent (3) <u>unspecified</u> elements from a set with two or more (4) <u>elements</u>. This set is called the (5) **replacement set** for the variable. A (6) **constant,** on the other hand, is a (7) <u>symbol</u> that names exactly one object. The symbol 8 is a constant, since it always names the number eight.

An (8) **algebraic expression** is a meaningful symbolic form involving constants, variables, (9) <u>mathematical operations</u>, and grouping symbols. For example,

$$2 + 8 \qquad 4 \cdot 3 - 7 \qquad 16 - 3(7 - 4)$$
$$5x - 3y \qquad 7(x + 2y) \qquad 4\{u - 3[u - 2(u + I)]\}$$

are all algebraic expressions.

Two or more algebraic expressions, each taken as a single (10) <u>entity</u> and joined by plus or minus signs, are called (11) **terms**. For good reasons, a term includes the sign that precedes it. Two or more algebraic expressions joined by multiplication are called (12) **factors.** For example,

$$
\begin{array}{cc}
\text{Factors} & \text{Factors} \\
\swarrow \downarrow & \swarrow \downarrow \\
\end{array}
$$
$$3\,(x - y) + (x + y)(x - y)$$
$$
\begin{array}{cc}
\text{Term} & \text{Term} \\
\end{array}
$$

has two terms, $3(x - y)$ and $(x + y)(x - y)$, and each of these terms has two factors. The first term has factors 3 and $(x - y)$, and the second term has factors $(x + y)$ and $(x - y)$. A term may contain several factors, and a factor may contain several terms.

Example 1

Terms and Factors

(13) <u>Identify</u> the terms and factors in the following algebraic expressions:

   (A) $3xy$ **(B)** $x + y - z - 3$ **(C)** $x(x - 1) + 2x$

Solution   **(A)** The expression has three factors: $3, x,$ and y.
   (B) The expression has four terms: $x, y, -z,$ and -3.
   (C) The expression consists of two terms: $x(x - 1)$ and $2x$. The first term has two factors, x and $x - 1$, and the second of these factors has two terms, namely x and -1. The second term, $2x$, has two factors, 2 and x.

Matched Problem I

Identify the terms and factors in the following algebraic expressions:

   (A) $a + b - 1$ **(B)** $23xyz$ **(C)** $x(x - 1)(x + y + 2)$

To (14) **evaluate** an algebraic expression for particular values of the variables means to replace each variable by a given value and then (15) <u>calculate</u> the resulting arithmetic value. Thus, for example, to evaluate $3xy$ when $x = 5$ and $y = 7$, we calculate

$$3xy = 3(5)(7) = 105$$

The introduction of variables into mathematics in the Western world occurred about AD 1600, although the basic idea had been developed earlier in India. A French mathematician, François Vieta (1540–1603), is singled out as the one mainly responsible for this new idea in the West. Many mark this point as the beginning of modern mathematics. Variables allow us to (16) <u>concisely</u> state general properties of numbers, such as

$$a + b = b + a \text{ for all numbers } a \text{ and } b$$

Variables also enable us to write statements about problem situations in (17) <u>compact</u> equations, such as

$$16 + 2x = 1 + 5x \quad \text{or} \quad 3x - 2(2x - 5) = 2(x + 3) - 8$$

All the work you will do in this text will relate in some way to algebraic expressions involving variables. You will be asked to (18) *translate* problem situations into algebraic expressions and equations involving them, to *rewrite* such expressions in different forms, to *evaluate* them, to (19) <u>solve</u> equations involving them, to *graph* equations and solutions to equations, and to *use* all of these skills to solve (20) <u>applied</u> problems.

Exercise 1: Summary

Before you begin to zero in on the underlined words in the passage, try to talk with a fellow student about the content of the passage. Then, in your own words, explain what an algebraic expression is, what a term is, and what a factor is.

_____

_____

_____

_____

_____

Exercise 2: Example

Write an algebraic expression, and identify the terms and factors in it.

_____

_____

_____

_____

_____

Exercise 3: Definitions

Working on your own or with a fellow student, try to define the underlined words from the selection you have just read. In many cases, you can find the definition in the text. The notation "(stated)" will tell you when this is so. For other terms, you will need to rely on the context and your own background knowledge. Write each definition in the space provided after the word.

1. equations

_____

2. variable (stated)

_____

3. unspecified

_____

4. elements

_____

5. replacement set

_____

6. constant (stated)

_____

7. symbol

_____

8. algebraic expression (stated)

_____

9. mathematical operations

_____

10. entity

_____

11. terms (stated)

_____

12. factors (stated)

_____

13. identify

_____

14. evaluate (stated)

_____

15. calculate

_____

16. concisely

_____

17. compact

_____

18. translate

_____

19. solve

_____

20. applied

_____

Now compare your answers to the definitions in the word list that follows. Since your definitions are written in your own words, they will probably be less formal and more understandable for you. Check to be sure that the content is essentially the same, but don't substitute the dictionary-type definitions for your own. You will find that learning definitions in your own words rather than memorizing the ones in the book will help you learn the meanings better and remember them longer.

WORD LIST

The words listed below are the ones that you are studying in this chapter. Although you have met them in the context of an algebra passage, you may find some of them in other types of textbooks, newspapers, magazines, professional journals, and recreational reading sources as well.

1. **algebraic expression** (al jə brā′ ik ek spre′ shən) a meaningful symbolic form involving constants, variables, mathematical operations, and grouping symbols.

2. **applied** (ə plīd), _adj._ having a practical purpose or dealing with actual phenomena.

3. **calculate** (kal′ kyə lāt), _v._ **1.** to determine by mathematical methods. **2.** to estimate. **3.** to compute. **4.** to reckon by practical methods.

4. **compact** (kəm pakt′), _adj._ **1.** dense, packed closely together. **2.** designed to be small in size and economical in operation.

5. **concise** (kən sīs′), _adj._ expressing much in a few words or symbols; brief; to the point.

6. **constant** (kon′ stənt), _n._ **1.** a symbol that names exactly one object. _adj._ **2.** steadfast; unchanging.

7. **element** (el′ ə ment), _n._ **1.** a member of a mathematical set. **2.** a constituent part. **3.** a fundamental principle. _(pl.)_ **4.** weather or atmospheric forces.

8. **entity** (en′ ti tē), _n._ something that exists in reality or independently.

9. **equation** (i kwā′ zhən), _n._ a mathematical expression asserting the equivalence of two quantities.

10. **evaluate** (i val′ yōō āt), *v.* **1.** to replace each variable by a given value and calculate the resulting arithmentic value. **2.** to judge or determine the value of.

11. **factor** (fak′ tər), *n.* **1.** two or more algebraic expressions joined by multiplication. **2.** one of the elements contributing to a situation.

12. **identify** (ī den′ tə fī), *v.* to recognize as being a particular person or thing.

13. **mathematical operation** (math ə mat′ ə kəl op ə rā′ shən) a process, such as addition, multiplication, or differentiation, performed according to specific rules.

14. **replacement set** (ri plās′ ment set) a group of objects or elements grouped together that are used to replace the variable in an equation.

15. **solve** (solv), *v.* to work out the answer to a problem.

16. **symbol** (sim′ bəl), *n.* a letter, character, or sign that represents a quantity, element, or operation.

17. **term** (tərm), *n.* each quantity in an algebraic expression connected by a plus or minus sign.

18. **translate** (trans′ lāt), *v.* **1.** to convey from one form to another. **2.** to express in terms that can be more easily understood.

19. **unspecified** (un spes′ ə fīd), *adj.* not specific, precise, or identified.

20. **variable** (ver′ ē ə bəl), *n.* a symbol used to represent any of a set of values.

Exercise 4: Matching

Match the terms in column A with their definitions in column B.

	Column A	*Column B*
_____ 1.	calculate	a. a meaningful symbolic form involving constants, variables, mathematical operations, and grouping symbols.
_____ 2.	equation	b. to recognize as being a particular thing
_____ 3.	identify	c. each element in an algebraic expression separated by a plus or minus sign
_____ 4.	solve	d. to express in different or simpler terms

_____ 5. concise

e. a group of objects used as substitutes in an algebraic expression

_____ 6. unspecified

f. brief, to the point

_____ 7. term

g. a mathematical expression that indicates the equivalence of two quantities

_____ 8. translate

h. to find the answer to a problem

_____ 9. replacement set

i. to determine by mathematical methods.

_____ 10. algebraic expression

j. not specific or precise

	Column A	*Column B*

_____ 11. evaluate

k. a symbol used to represent unspecified elements from a set

_____ 12. compact

l. two or more algebraic expressions joined by multiplication

_____ 13. element

m. to express in more understandable terms

_____ 14. factor

n. something that exists independently

_____ 15. variable

o. a symbol that names one specific object

_____ 16. applied

p. to calculate the arithmetic value

_____ 17. entity

q. a letter, character, or sign that represents a quantity, element, or an operation

_____ 18. constant

r. having a useful purpose

_____ 19. translate

s. dense

_____ 20. symbol

t. a member of a mathematical set

Exercise 5: Fill-In

Choose the word that best completes each sentence below and write its letter in the space provided.

a. unspecified   d. concisely   g. applied   i. elements
b. identify   e. translate   h. solve   j. calculate
c. entity   f. compact

_____ 1. Members of the selection committee congratulated the representative of the advertising agency for stating her proposal so _____ .

_____ 2. The pharmaceutical company hires scientists specifically for _____ research related to their products.

_____ 3. Although the victim was unable to _____ his attackers, he provided a very specific description of their car.

_____ 4. Soon after arriving in this country, Soo Ying learned English so quickly that friends often asked her to _____ for them.

_____ 5. One phrase in his job description disturbed Juan—"plus any other _____ duties requested by the manager."

_____ 6. Chiquita worried that she would not be able to _____ fifteen math problems in the allotted time of one hour.

_____ 7. Living in a small apartment in the city, Liz makes it a point to purchase _____ appliances and furniture that take up the least space.

_____ 8. The realtor showed Tom and Carol how to _____ the differences in their monthly payments according to the interest rate.

_____ 9. The alphabet can be considered a set with twenty-six _____ that are the letters.

_____ 10. In a term, each algebraic expression is treated as a single _____ .

Exercise 6: Application

Write your own examples of the following:

1.   an algebraic expression

   _____

2.   a constant

   _____

3.   a factor

   _____

4.   a term

   _____

5.   an equation

   _____

LITERATURE: "A ROSE FOR EMILY"

10

Students who major in liberal arts or humanities study literature, sometimes as part of their English composition courses and sometimes in courses devoted exclusively to literature. Many instructors of such courses choose an anthology that contains many different pieces of literature or excerpts from them. The story you will read in this chapter, "A Rose for Emily," is found in many anthologies. Although the words you will study are all found in the first section of the story, the entire story is printed in the hope that you will enjoy reading on till the end. There are many reasons to study literature, but one of the most important is enjoyment. A "good story" should have an interesting plot or characters, should convey some sort of a message, should engage the reader, and should have application beyond the details of the story. At times, students are put off by language that seems different from their own in either word choice or unfamiliar expressions. You will notice that this story contains quite a few words you might not be able to define in isolation. In the context of the story, however, you need not resort to your dictionary each time you come across an unfamiliar word. Use the context and the flow of the story line to help you with words you may not know. Discuss the plot and characters with your fellow students. You might also choose to try the question that follows the story, to explore it from a literary view as well as to make use of an opportunity to increase your vocabulary.

Read the following story to enjoy it and to learn about Miss Emily.

WILLIAM FAULKNER
[1897–1962]
"A Rose for Emily"

I

When Miss Emily Grierson died, our whole town went to her funeral: the men through a sort of respectful affection for a fallen (1) <u>monument</u>, the women mostly out of curiosity to see the inside of her house, which no one (2) <u>save</u> an old manservant—a combined gardener and cook—had seen in at least ten years.

It was a big, squarish frame house that had once been white, decorated with (3) <u>cupolas</u> and (4) <u>spires</u> and scrolled balconies in the heavily lightsome style of the seventies, set on what had once been our most select street. But garages and cotton gins had (5) <u>encroached</u> and (6) <u>obliterated</u> even the (7) <u>august</u> names of that neighborhood; only Miss Emily's house was left, lifting its stubborn and (8) <u>coquettish</u> decay above the cotton wagons and the gasoline pumps—an (9) <u>eyesore</u> among eyesores. And now Miss Emily had gone to join the representatives of those august names where they lay in the cedar (10) <u>bemused</u> cemetery among the ranked and anonymous graves of Union and Confederate soldiers who fell at the battle of Jefferson.

Alive, Miss Emily had been a tradition, a duty, and a care; a sort of hereditary obligation upon the town, dating from that day in 1894 when Colonel Sartoris, the mayor—he who fathered the (11) <u>edict</u> that no Negro woman should appear on the streets without an apron—(12) <u>remitted</u> her taxes, the (13) <u>dispensation</u> dating from the death of her father on into (14) <u>perpetuity</u>. Not that Miss Emily would have accepted charity. Colonel Sartoris invented an involved tale to the effect that Miss Emily's father had loaned money to the town, which the town, as a matter of business, preferred this way of repaying. Only a man of Colonel Sartoris' generation and thought could have invented it, and only a woman could have believed it.

When the next generation, with its more modern ideas, became mayors and aldermen, this arrangement created some little dissatisfaction. On the first day of the year they mailed her a tax notice. February came, and there was no reply. They wrote her a formal letter, asking her to call at the sheriff's office at her convenience. A week later the mayor wrote her himself, offering to send his car for her, and received in reply a note on paper of an (15) <u>archaic</u> shape, in a thin, flowing (16) <u>calligraphy</u> in faded ink, to the effect that she no longer went out at all. The tax notice was also enclosed, without comment.

They called a special meeting of the Board of Aldermen. A (17) <u>deputation</u> waited upon her, knocked at the door through which no visitor had passed since she ceased giving china-painting lessons eight or ten years earlier. They were admitted by the old Negro into a dim hall from which a stairway mounted into still more shadow. It smelled of dust and disuse—a close, dank smell. The Negro led them into the parlor. It was furnished in heavy, leather-covered furniture. When the Negro opened the blinds of one window, they could see that the leather was cracked, and when they sat down, a faint dust rose sluggishly about their thighs, spinning with slow (18) <u>motes</u> in the single sun-ray. On a tarnished (19) <u>gilt</u> easel before the fireplace stood a crayon portrait of Miss Emily's father.

They rose when she entered—a small, fat woman in black, with a thin gold chain descending to her waist and vanishing into her belt, leaning on an ebony cane with a tarnished gold head. Her skeleton was small and spare; perhaps that was why what would have been merely plumpness in another was obesity in her. She looked bloated, like a body long submerged in motionless water, and of that pallid (20) <u>hue</u>. Her eyes, lost in the fatty ridges of her face, looked like two small pieces of coal pressed into a lump of dough as they moved from one face to another while the visitors stated their errand.

Her voice was dry and cold. "I have no taxes in Jefferson. Colonel Sartoris explained it to me. Perhaps you can gain access to the city records and satisfy yourselves."

"But we have. We are the city authorities, Miss Emily. Didn't you get a notice from the sheriff, signed by him?"

"I received a paper, yes," Miss Emily said. "Perhaps he considers himself the sheriff. I have no taxes in Jefferson."

"But there is nothing on the books to show that, you see. We must go by the—"

"See Colonel Sartoris. I have no taxes in Jefferson."

"But, Miss Emily—"

"See Colonel Sartoris." (Colonel Sartoris had been dead almost ten years.) "I have no taxes in Jefferson. Tobe!" The Negro appeared. "Show these gentlemen out."

2

So she vanquished them, hose and foot, just as she had vanquished their fathers thirty years before about the smell. That was two years after her father's death and a short time after her sweetheart—the one we believed would marry her—had deserted her. After her father's death, she went out very little; after her sweetheart went away, people hardly saw her at all. A few of the ladies had the temerity to call, but were not received, and the only sign of life about the place was the Negro man— a young man then—going in and out with a market basket.

"Just as if a man—any man—could keep a kitchen properly," the ladies said; so they were not surprised when the smell developed. It was another link between the gross, teeming world and the high and mighty Griersons.

A neighbor, a woman, complained to the mayor, Judge Stevens, eighty years old.

"But what will you have me do about it, madam?" he said.

"Why, send her word to stop it," the woman said. "Isn't there a law?"

"I'm sure that won't be necessary," Judge Stevens said. "It's probably just a snake or a rat that nigger of hers killed in the yard. I'll speak to him about it."

The next day he received two more complaints, one from a man who came in diffident deprecation. "We really must do something about it, Judge. I'd be the last one in the world to bother Miss Emily, but we've got to do something." That night the Board of Aldermen met—three graybeards and one younger man, a member of the rising generation.

"It's simple enough," he said. "Send her word to have her place cleaned up. Give her a certain time to do it in, and if she don't . . ."

"Dammit, sir," Judge Stevens said, "will you accuse a lady to her face of smelling bad?"

So the next night, after midnight, four men crossed Miss Emily's lawn and slunk about the house, like burglars, sniffing along the base of the brickwork and at the cellar openings while one of them performed a regular sowing motion with his hand out of a sack slung from his shoulder. They broke open the cellar door and sprinkled lime there, and in all the outbuildings. As they recrossed the lawn, a window that had been dark was lighted and Miss Emily sat in it, the light behind her, and her upright torso motionless as that of an idol. They crept quietly across the lawn and into the shadow of the locusts that lined the street. After a week or two the smell went away.

That was when people began to feel really sorry for her. People in our town, remembering how old lady Wyatt, her great-aunt, had gone completely crazy at last, believed that the Griersons held themselves a little too high for what they really were. None of the young men were quite good enough for Miss Emily and such. We had long thought of them as a tableau, Miss Emily a slender figure in white in the background, her father a spaddled silhouette in the foreground, his back to her and clutching a horsewhip, the two of them framed by the back-flung front door. So when she got to be thirty and was still single, we were not pleased exactly, but vindicated; even with insanity in the family she wouldn't have turned down all of her chances if they had really materialized.

When her father died, it got about that the house was all that was left to her; and in a way, people were glad. At last they could pity Miss Emily. Being left alone, and a pauper, she had become humanized. Now she too would know the old thrill and the old despair of a penny more or less.

The day after his death all the ladies prepared to call at the house and offer condolence and aid, as is our custom. Miss Emily met them at the door, dressed as usual and with no trace of grief on her face. She told them that her father was not dead. She did that for three days, with the ministers calling on her, and the doctors, trying to persuade her to let them dispose of the body. Just as they were about to resort to law and force, she broke down, and they buried her father quickly.

We did not say she was crazy then. We believed she had to do that. We remembered all the young men her father had driven away, and we knew that with nothing left, she would have to cling to that which had robbed her, as people will.

3

She was sick for a long time. When we saw her again, her hair was cut short, making her look like a girl, with a vague resemblance to those angels in colored church windows—sort of tragic and serene.

The town had just let the contracts for paving the sidewalks, and in the summer after her father's death they began the work. The construction company came with niggers and mules and machinery, and a foreman named Homer Barron, a Yankee—a big, dark, ready man, with a big voice and eyes lighter than his face. The little boys would follow in groups to hear him cuss the niggers, and the niggers singing in time to the rise and fall of picks. Pretty soon he knew everybody in town. Whenever you heard a lot of laughing anywhere about the square, Homer Barron would be in the center of the group. Presently, we began to see him and Miss Emily on Sunday afternoons driving in the yellow-wheeled buggy and the matched team of bays from the livery stable.

At first we were glad that Miss Emily would have an interest, because the ladies all said, "Of course a Grierson would not think seriously of a Northerner, a day laborer." But there were still others, older people, who said that even grief could not cause a real lady to forget *noblesse oblige*—without calling it *noblesse oblige*. They just said, "Poor Emily. Her kinfolk should come to her." She had some kin in Alabama; but years ago her father had fallen out with them over the estate of old lady Wyatt, the crazy woman, and there was no communication between the two families. They had not even been represented at the funeral.

And as soon as the old people said, "Poor Emily," the whispering began. "Do you suppose it's really so?" they said to one another. "Of course it is. What else could . . ." This behind their hands; rustling of craned silk and satin behind jalousies closed upon the sun of Sunday afternoon as the thin, swift clop-clop-clop of the matched team passed: "Poor Emily."

She carried her head high enough—even when we believed that she was fallen. It was as if she demanded more than ever the recognition of her dignity as the last Grierson; as if it had wanted that touch of earthiness to reaffirm her imperviousness. Like when she bought the rat poison, the arsenic. That was over a year after they had begun to say "Poor Emily," and while the two female cousins were visiting her.

"I want some poison," she said to the druggist. She was over thirty then, still a slight woman, though thinner than usual, with cold, haughty black eyes in a face the flesh of which was strained across the temples and about the eye sockets as you imagine a lighthouse-keeper's face ought to look. "I want some poison," she said.

"Yes, Miss Emily. What kind? For rats and such? I'd recom—"

"I want the best you have. I don't care what kind."

The druggist named several. "They'll kill anything up to an elephant. But what you want is—"

"Arsenic," Miss Emily said. "Is that a good one?"

"Is . . . arsenic? Yes, Ma'am. But what you want—"

"I want arsenic."

The druggist looked down at her. She looked back at him, erect, her face like a strained flag. "Why, of course," the druggist said. "If that's what you want. But the law requires you to tell what you are going to use it for."

Miss Emily just stared at him, her head tilted back in order to look him eye for eye, until he looked away and went and got the arsenic and wrapped it up. The Negro delivery boy brought her the package; the druggist didn't come back. When she opened the package at home there was written on the box, under the skull and bones: "For rats."

<h2 style="text-align:center">4</h2>

So the next day we all said, "She will kill herself"; and we said it would be the best thing. When she had first begun to be seen with Homer Barron, we had said, "She will marry him." Then we said, "She will persuade him yet," because Homer himself had remarked—he liked men, and it was known that he drank with the younger men in the Elks' Club—that he was not a marrying man. Later we said, "Poor Emily" behind the jalousies as they passed on Sunday afternoon in the glittering buggy, Miss Emily with her head high and Homer Barron with his hat cocked and a cigar in his teeth, reins and whip in a yellow glove.

Then some of the ladies began to say that it was a disgrace to the town and a bad example to the young people. The men did not want to interfere, but at last the ladies forced the Baptist minister—Miss Emily's people were Episcopal—to call upon her. He would never divulge what happened during that interview, but he refused to go back again. The next Sunday they again drove the streets, and the following day the minister's wife wrote to Miss Emily's relations in Alabama.

So she had blood-kin under her roof again and we sat back to watch developments. At first nothing happened. Then we were sure they were to be married. We learned that Miss Emily had been to the jeweler's and ordered a man's toilet set in silver, with the letters H.B. on each piece. Two days later we learned that she had bought a complete outfit of men's clothing, including a nightshirt, and we said, "They are married." We were really glad. We were glad because the two female cousins were even more Grierson than Miss Emily had ever been.

So we were not surprised when Homer Barron—the streets had been finished some time since—was gone. We were a little disappointed that there was not a public blowing-off, but we believed that he had gone on to prepare for Miss Emily's coming, or to give her a chance to get rid of the cousins. (By that time it was a cabal, and we were all Miss Emily's allies to help circumvent the cousins.) Sure enough, after another week they departed. And, as we had expected all along, within three days Homer Barron was back in town. A neighbor saw the Negro man admit him at the kitchen door at dusk one evening.

And that was the last we saw of Homer Barron. And of Miss Emily for some time. The Negro man went in and out with the market basket, but the front door remained closed. Now and then we would see her at the window for a moment, as the men did that night when they sprinkled the lime, but for almost six months she did not appear on the streets. Then we knew that this was to be expected too; as if that quality of her father that had thwarted her woman's life so many times had been too virulent and too furious to die.

When we next saw Miss Emily, she had grown fat and her hair was turning gray. During the next few years it grew grayer and grayer until it attained an even pepper-and-salt iron-gray, when it ceased turning. Up to the day of her death at seventy-four it was still that vigorous iron-gray, like the hair of an active man.

From that time on her front door remained closed, save during a period of six or seven years, when she was about forty, during which she gave lessons in china-painting. She fitted up a studio in one of the downstairs rooms, where the daughters and granddaughters of Colonel Sartoris' contemporaries were sent to her with the same regularity and in the same spirit that they were sent to church on Sundays with a twenty-five-cent piece for the collection plate. Meanwhile her taxes had been remitted.

Then the newer generation became the backbone and the spirit of the town, and the painting pupils grew up and fell away and did not send their children to her with boxes of color and tedious brushes and pictures cut from the ladies' magazines. The front door closed upon the last one and remained closed for good. When the town got free postal delivery, Miss Emily alone refused to let them fasten the metal numbers above her door and attach a mailbox to it. She would not listen to them.

Daily, monthly, yearly we watched the Negro grow grayer and more stooped, going in and out with the market basket. Each December we sent her a tax notice, which would be returned by the post office a week later, unclaimed. Now and then we would see her in one of the downstairs windows—she had evidently shut up the top floor of the house—like the carven torso of an idol in a niche, looking or not looking at us, we could never tell which. Thus she passed from generation to generation—dear, inescapable, impervious, tranquil, and perverse.

And so she died. Fell ill in the house filled with dust and shadows, with only a doddering Negro man to wait on her. We did not even know she was sick; we had long since given up trying to get any information from the Negro. He talked to no one, probably not even to her, for his voice had grown harsh and rusty, as if from disuse.

She died in one of the downstairs rooms, in a heavy walnut bed with a curtain, her gray head propped on a pillow yellow and moldy with age and lack of sunlight.

5

The Negro met the first of the ladies at the front door and let them in, with their hushed, sibilant voices and their quick, curious glances, and then he disappeared. He walked right through the house and out the back and was not seen again.

The two female cousins came at once. They held the funeral on the second day, with the town coming to look at Miss Emily beneath a mass of bought flowers, with the crayon face of her father musing profoundly above the bier and the ladies sibilant and macabre; and the very old men—some in their brushed Confederate uniforms—on the porch and the lawn, talking of Miss Emily as if she had been a contemporary of theirs, believing that they had danced with her and courted her perhaps, confusing time with its mathematical progression, as the old do, to whom all the past is not a diminishing road but, instead, a huge meadow which no winter ever quite touches, divided from them now by the narrow bottleneck of the most recent decade of years.

Already we knew that there was one room in that region above stairs which no one had seen in forty years, and which would have to be forced. They waited until Miss Emily was decently in the ground before they opened it.

The violence of breaking down the door seemed to fill this room with pervading dust. A thin, acrid pall as of the tomb seemed to lie everywhere upon this room decked and furnished as if for a bridal: upon the valance curtains of faded rose color, upon the rose-shaded lights, upon the dressing table, upon the delicate array of crystal and the man's toilet things backed with tarnished silver, silver so tarnished that the monogram was obscured. Among them lay a collar and tie, as if they had just been removed, which, lifted, left upon the surface a pale crescent in the dust. Upon a chair hung the suit, carefully folded; beneath it the two mute shoes and the discarded socks.

The man himself lay in the bed.

For a long while we just stood there, looking down at the profound and fleshless grin. The body had apparently once lain in the attitude of an embrace, but now the long sleep that outlasts love, that conquers even the grimace of love, had cuckolded him. What was left of him, rotted beneath what was left of the nightshirt, had become inextricable from the bed in which he lay; and upon him and upon the pillow beside him lay that even coating of the patient and biding dust.

Then we noticed that in the second pillow was the indentation of a head. One of us lifted something from it, and leaning forward, that faint and invisible dust dry and acrid in the nostrils, we saw a long strand of iron-gray hair.

QUESTION

Although "A Rose for Emily" is narrated in the first person, the narrator is not "I" but "we." The narrator thus represents a communal rather than an individual point of view. How does the narrator (and the town) view Miss Emily? Find passages that represent more than one view of her, and explain their significance.

Exercise 1: Summary

Before you begin to zero in on the underlined words in the story, try to talk with a fellow student about the plot and the characters. Then, in your own words, describe Miss Emily and her relationship with the town.

_____

_____

_____

_____

_____

Exercise 2: Example

Describe someone you know (or have heard about or read about) who lives alone. Tell what that person's relationship is to his or her neighbors.

_____

_____

_____

_____

Exercise 3: Definitions

Working on your own or with a fellow student, try to define the underlined words from the selection you have just read. You will need to rely on the context and your own background knowledge. Note that some of the words in this story are used in a different way than you may be used to. Define them according to how they are used in the story. Write each definition in the space provided after the word.

1. monument

_____

2. save

_____

3. cupolas

_____

4. spires

_____

5. encroached

_____

6. obliterated

_____

7. august

_____

8. coquettish

_____

9. eyesore

_____

10. bemused

_____

11. edict

_____

12. remitted

_____

13. dispensation

_____

14. perpetuity

_____

15. archaic

_____

16. calligraphy

_____

17. deputation

_____

18. motes

_____

19. gilt

_____

20. hue

_____

Now compare your answers to the definitions in the word list that follows. Since your definitions are written in your own words, they will probably be less formal and more understandable for you. Check to be sure that the content is essentially the same, but don't substitute the dictionary-type definitions for your own. You will find that learning definitions in your own words rather than memorizing the ones in the book will help you learn the meanings better and remember them longer.

WORD LIST

The words listed below are the ones that you are studying in this chapter. Although you have met them in the context of a literary passage, you may find some of them in other types of textbooks, newspapers, magazines, professional journals, and recreational reading sources as well.

1. **archaic** (är kā′ ik) belonging to an earlier time; not current or modern.

2. **august** (ô gust′), *adj.* inspiring respect, reverence, or awe.

3. **bemuse** (bē myōōz′), *v.* to confuse or bewilder.

4. **calligraphy** (kə lig′ rə fē), *n.* fancy or elegant handwriting.

5. **coquettish** (kō ket′ ish), *adj.* flirtatious; describing behavior designed to attract the attention of the opposite sex.

6. **cupola** (kyōō′ pə lə), *n.* a small, domelike structure on top of a roof that may contain a bell or a light.

7. **deputation** (dep yə tā′ shən), *n.* a person, a group, or a delegation appointed to act as representative for others.

8. **dispensation** (dis pen sā′ shən), *n.* an exemption or release from a rule or an obligation.

9. **edict** (ē′ dikt), *n.* an order, a proclamation, or a decree.

10. **encroach** (en krōch′), *v.* to trespass or intrude on the rights or property of others.

11. **eyesore** (ī′ sôr), *n.* something unpleasant or offensive to look at.

12. **gilt** (gilt), *adj.* coated with gold material or color.

13. **hue** (hyōō), *n.* color or shade.

14. **monument** (mon′ yə ment), *n.* **1.** an exceptional or heroic person. **2.** a statue or other structure erected as a memorial. 3. a lasting reminder.

15. **mote** (mōt), *n.* a small particle or speck.

16. **obliterate** (ə blit' ər āt), *v.* to destroy, leaving no traces; to wipe out, cover up, or erase.

17. **perpetuity** (pûr pi tōō' i tē), *n.* the quality of being everlasting or endless.

18. **remit** (ri mit'), *v.* **1.** to pardon, forgive, or excuse from an obligation or penalty. **2.** to send money.

19. **save** (sāv), *prep.* **1.** except or but. *v.* **2.** to rescue from harm. **3.** to keep safe. **3.** to refrain from spending. **4.** to treat carefully to avoid wear or damage. **5.** to copy onto a computer disk. **6.** to redeem from sin. **7.** to keep a ball or puck from entering one's goal.

20. **spire** (spīr), *n.* a tall, slender pointed structure on a roof or tower.

Exercise 4: Matching

Match the terms in column A with their definitions in column B.

	Column A	*Column B*
_____ 1.	gilt	a. a small structure on a roof
_____ 2.	archaic	b. a delegation of representatives
_____ 3.	encroach	c. something unattractive
_____ 4.	edict	d. golden
_____ 5.	august	e. to trespass or intrude
_____ 6.	cupola	f. a forgiveness or pardon from a duty
_____ 7.	deputation	g. old-fashioned
_____ 8.	monument	h. a decree or proclamation
_____ 9.	eyesore	i. heroic, inspiring reverence
_____ 10.	dispensation	j. an admirable person or a memorial

	Column A	*Column B*
_____ 11.	mote	k. to wipe out
_____ 12.	remit	l. flirtatious
_____ 13.	save	m. fancy handwriting

_____ 14.	perpetuity	n. a speck or particle
_____ 15.	calligraphy	o. to confuse or bewilder
_____ 16.	hue	p. to excuse
_____ 17.	spire	q. except
_____ 18.	coquettish	r. forever
_____ 19.	bemuse	s. a pointed structure on a roof
_____ 20.	obliterate	t. a shade of a color

Exercise 5: Fill-In

Choose the word that best completes each sentence below and write its letter in the space provided.

a. encroach	d. obliterated	g. monument	i. bemused
b. calligraphy	e. perpetuity	h. archaic	j. eyesore
c. hue	f. cupola		

_____ 1. The planning board denied the Dixons' application for a garage permit since the proposed structure would

_____ on their neighbor's property.

_____ 2. After the hurricane struck the island, the town hall and

police station were completely _____ .

_____ 3. Neighbors considered the abandoned park an _____ with its rusting and broken playground equipment.

_____ 4. Irena's grandmother's ideas and language seemed so

_____ to her that she rarely enjoyed her visits.

_____ 5. Laura's friend who is skilled in _____ offered to address her wedding invitations.

_____ 6. The architect recommended a _____ to break up the long, straight roofline.

_____ 7. Carlos's _____ expression indicated that the conversation at the party was going too fast for him to follow.

_____ 8. Laquane, the prom chairperson, chose blue as the theme

color and selected her dress in a very pale _____ .

_____ 9. Thanks to years of volunteer work, the president of the PTA

was considered a _____ to the community.

_____ 10. After her parents' funerals, Akisha arranged with a local
florist to have flowers placed on the grave on their birthdays

into _____.

Exercise 6: Application

Create a dialogue that might have occurred between Miss Emily and the
Baptist minister sent to speak with her about her behavior.

_____

_____

_____

_____

_____

COMPUTER TECHNOLOGY: HOW TO SURF THE NET

11

In this chapter, you will read about the Internet and learn what it can do for you. First you will read an excerpt from an introductory computer technology text. Some of the terms in the reading will be numbered and underlined. (Many will also be printed in **boldface type** as they appeared in the original text.) Your first task will be to define them either from context or from the stated definition. In the exercises that follow, you will practice using the terms.

Computer technology is a field that is growing and changing rapidly. Many computer instructors do not use textbooks because they become outdated so quickly. Rather, they distribute handouts that allow students to learn the most current information, or they rely on software to teach their students. Introductory courses, though, provide basic information that has remained fairly stable. Students who are beginning to study about computers must learn the terminology that is used in the computer field so they can communicate in this information age. If you are interested in pursuing a career in computer technology, you may become a programmer who designs software to meet the specific needs of users or clients. Or you may help a specific company determine how to use computer technology to run its business more efficiently. Many computer experts are freelance consultants who move from one project to another. Even if you do not plan to enter the computer profession, most jobs in the future will require some knowledge of and familiarity with computers. More and more people find themselves using computers in their personal as well as their professional lives.

Read the following selection for an overview of the Internet and some examples of how we can use it.

THE INTERNET GUIDE: HOW TO SURF THE NET

The (1) <u>Internet</u> is like a highway that connects you to millions of other people and organizations. Unlike typical highways that move people and things from one place to another, the Internet moves your *ideas* and *information*. Rather than moving through geographic space, you move through (2) **cyberspace**—the space of electronic movement of ideas and information. In this guide, we describe the Internet, how you can get onto it, and how you can use it.

The Internet

THE INTERNET IS A GIANT WORLDWIDE NETWORK. POPULAR USES INCLUDE COMMUNICATING, SHOPPING, RESEARCHING, AND ENTERTAINMENT.

The Internet is a giant worldwide network. It connects computer systems located throughout the world that are willing to share their resources. The Internet has created a cooperative society that forms a (3) <u>virtual</u> community stretching from one end of the globe to the other.

The Internet's origin can be traced back to 1969, when the United States government funded a major research project on computer networking. A national computer network called **ARPANET (Advanced Research Project Agency Network)** was developed. It was used by government and military agencies to communicate and share computer resources with researchers working on national security projects.

From these military and research beginnings, the Internet has evolved as a tool for all of us to use. Every day more than 30 million people in over 50 countries use the Internet. By the year 2000, over a billion users from every country in the world are expected to be connected to the Internet.

To access the Internet, you connect to one of the computer systems already on it. After you connect to one, you can easily connect to another. You may move electronically from one computer system to another, from one site to another, and often from one country to another—all within seconds. What makes the Internet so remarkable is the incredible speed and efficiency with which these connections are made. Once you are on the Internet it seems like you are on a single giant computer that branches all over the world.

Internet Applications

What can you do on the Internet? There are any number of uses for the Internet. The most common are:

- **Communicating:** Sending and receiving e-mail is the most popular Internet activity. You can send and receive e-mail to and from your friends and family located almost anywhere in the world. You can join and listen to discussions on a wide variety of special-interest topics.
- **Shopping:** One of the fastest-growing (4) <u>applications</u> is electronic commerce. You can visit a cyber mall to window shop at the best stores, look for the latest fashions, search for bargains, and make purchases.
- **Researching:** How would you like to have one of the world's largest libraries available from home? Well, you can have several of them.
- **Entertainment:** Do you like music, the movies, reading, or playing computer games? You'll find them all on the Internet waiting for you to locate and enjoy.

Where should you begin to learn more about how to use and to (5) <u>surf</u> the Internet? First, you should gain access to or get onto the Internet. Then, explore the applications and use the Internet services. The following sections of the guide will help you do just that.

Access

Providers give access to the Internet. Internet connections are either direct, SLIP and PPP, or terminal connection. Protocols are rules for exchanging information between computers.

The Internet and the telephone system are similar—you can connect to the Internet much like you connect a phone to the telephone system. Once you are on the Internet, your computer becomes an extension of what seems like a giant computer—a computer that branches all over the world.

Providers

The most common way to access the Internet is through a (6) **provider** or **host computer**. The providers are already connected to the Internet and provide a path or connection for individuals to access the Internet. There are two widely used providers.

- **Colleges and universities:** Most colleges and universities provide free access to the Internet through their local area networks. You may be able to access the Internet through your school or through other local colleges and universities.

- **Service providers:** A widely used source for access is through (7) **Internet service providers (ISPs)**. National service providers provide access to the Internet and numerous other electronic services for a fee. The best-known are America Online and Microsoft Network. Local service providers are available in many areas. Typically, they cost less and provide fewer services.

Connections

To gain access to the Internet, you must have a connection. This connection can be made either directly to the Internet or indirectly through a provider. There are three types of connections:

- **Direct or dedicated:** To have efficient access to all the functions on the Internet, you need a (8) direct or dedicated link. Individuals rarely have direct connections because they are quite expensive. However, many organizations such as colleges, universities, service providers, and corporations do have direct links.

    The primary advantages of a direct link are complete access to Internet functions, ease of connection for individual users, and fast response and (9) retrieval of information. The primary disadvantage is cost.

- **SLIP and PPP:** Using a high-speed (10) modem and standard telephone lines, you can connect to a provider that has a direct connection to the Internet. This type of connection requires special software such as (11) **SLIP (serial line internet protocol)** or **PPP (point to point protocol)**. Using this type of connection, your computer becomes part of a client/server network. The provider or host computer is the server providing access to the Internet. Your computer is the client. Using special client software, your computer is able to communicate with server software running on the provider's computer and on other Internet computers.

    This type of connection is widely used by end users to connect to the Internet. It provides a high level of service at a lower cost than a direct or dedicated connection. Of course, it is somewhat slower and may not be as convenient.

- **Terminal connection:** Another way to access the Internet using a high-speed modem and standard telephone lines is called a (12) **terminal connection**. Using this type of connection, your computer becomes a part of a terminal network. Unlike a SLIP or PPP connection, your computer's operations are very limited. It operates as a terminal that simply displays the communication that occurs between the provider and the other computers on the Internet. Compared to a SLIP or PPP connection, terminal connection is less expensive but not as fast or convenient.

TCP/IP

When information is sent over the Internet, it usually travels through numerous interconnected networks. Before a message is sent, it is broken down into small parts called (13) **packets.** Each packet is then sent separately over the Internet, possibly traveling different routes to one common destination. At the receiving end, the packets are reassembled into the correct order. Protocols control how the messages are broken down, sent, and reassembled. They govern how and when computers talk to one another. The standard protocol for the Internet is called (14) **TCP/IP (transmission control protocol/internet protocol).**

E-Mail

An e-mail message has three basic elements. Internet addresses use the domain name system. E-mail etiquette is called netiquette.

(15) **E-mail** is a way of sending an electronic letter or message between individuals or computers. It is like an answering machine in that you can receive messages even when you are not at home. Unlike an answering machine, e-mail can contain text, graphics, and images as well as sound. E-mail can also be used to communicate with more than one person at a time, to conveniently schedule meetings, to keep current on important events, and much more.

Sending and receiving e-mail is by far the most common Internet activity. You can communicate with anyone in the world who has an Internet address or e-mail account with a system connected to the Internet. E-mail programs such as Pine, Elm, and Eudora automate the process of creating, sending, reading, and receiving messages.

Suppose that you have a friend, Chris James, who is going to an out-of-state college. You and Chris have been calling back and forth at least once a week for the past month. Unfortunately, your telephone bill has skyrocketed. Fortunately, you both have Internet e-mail accounts through your schools. To save money, you and Chris agree to communicate via the Internet instead of the telephone. After exchanging e-mail addresses, you are ready to send your first Internet e-mail message to Chris.

Basic Elements

A typical e-mail message has three basic elements: header, message, and signature. The header appears first and typically includes the following information.

Figure 5

Basic elements of an e-mail message.

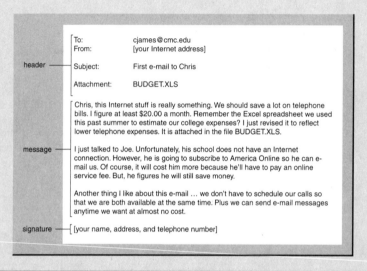

- **To line:** The e-mail address for the person that is to receive the letter.
- **From line:** The address of the person sending the e-mail follows the To line.
- **Subject line:** A one-line description of the message is used to present the topic of the message. Subject lines typically are displayed when a person checks his or her mailbox.
- **Attachment line:** Many e-mail programs allow you to attach files such as documents and worksheets. If a message has an attachment, the file name appears on the attachment line.

The letter or message comes next. It is typically short and to the point. Finally the signature line provides additional information about the sender. Typically, this information includes the sender's name, address, and telephone number.

Addresses

One of the most important elements of an e-mail message is the address of the person who is to receive the letter. The Internet uses an addressing method known as the (16) **domain name system (DNS)** to

Figure 6
Parts of an Internet address.

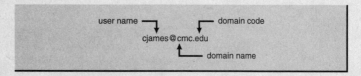

Figure 7
Commonly used Internet domain codes.

DOMAIN	IDENTIFICATION
com	Commercial
edu	Educational and research
gov	Government
mil	Military
net	Major network centers
org	Other organizations

DOMAIN CODES

assign names and numbers to people and computers. This system divides an address into three parts.

Internet addresses typically are read backwards. The last part of the address is the (17) **domain code**, which identifies the geographical description or organizational identification. For example, *edu* indicates an address at an educational or research institution.

Separated from the domain code by a dot (.) is the (18) **domain name.** It is a reference to the particular organization. In this case, *cmc* represents Claremont McKenna College. Separated from the domain name by an "at" (@) symbol, the (19) **user name** identifies a unique person or computer at the listed domain. The address shown in figure 6 is for Chris James (cjames) at Claremont McKenna College (cmc), which is an education and research institution (edu).

Figure 8
E-mail etiquette.

NETIQUETTE

1. Don't send abusive, threatening, harassing, or bigoted messages. You could be held criminally liable for what you write.

2. DO NOT TYPE YOUR MESSAGES IN ALL UPPERCASE CHARACTERS! This is called shouting and is perceived as very harsh. Use a normal combination of upper- and lowercase characters. Sometimes all lowercase is perceived as too informal or timid.

3. Keep line length to 60 characters or less so your messages can be comfortably displayed on most monitors.

4. Before sending a message, carefully check the spelling, punctuation, and grammar. Also think twice about the content of your message. Once it is sent, you can't get it back.

Netiquette

(20) Netiquette refers to the etiquette you should observe when using e-mail. Remember that you are communicating with people, not computers—these people have the same feelings and sensibilities that you do.

Exercise 1: Summary

Before you begin to zero in on the underlined words in the passage, try to talk with a fellow student about the content of the passage. Then, in your own words, write a brief summary of what you have learned about how the Internet works and what its uses are.

_____

_____

_____

_____

_____

Exercise 2: Example

Give an example of a situation in which you use the Internet now or can imagine yourself using it in the future.

_____

_____

_____

_____

_____

Exercise 3: Definitions

Working on your own or with a fellow student, try to define the underlined words from the selection you have just read. In many cases, you can find the definition in the text. The notation "(stated)" will tell you when this is so. For other terms, you will need to rely on the context and your own background knowledge. Write each definition in the space provided after the word.

1. Internet

   _____

2. cyberspace (stated)

   _____

3. virtual

   _____

4. applications

   _____

5. surf

   _____

6. provider or host computer

   _____

7. Internet service providers (ISP) (stated)

   _____

8. direct or dedicated link (stated)

   _____

9. retrieval

_____

10. modem

_____

11. SLIP (serial line internet protocol) or PPP (point to point protocol)
(stated)

_____

12. terminal connection (stated)

_____

13. packets (stated)

_____

14. TCP/IP (transmission control protocol/internet protocol) (stated)

_____

15. e-mail (stated)

_____

16. domain name system (DNS) (stated)

_____

17. domain code (stated)

_____

18. domain name (stated)

_____

19. user name (stated)

_____

20. netiquette (stated)

_____

Now compare your answers to the definitions in the word list that follows. Since your definitions are written in your own words, they will probably be less formal and more understandable for you. Check to be sure that the content is essentially the same, but don't substitute the dictionary-type definitions for your own. You will find that learning definitions in your own words rather than memorizing the ones in the book will help you learn the meanings better and remember them longer.

WORD LIST

The words listed below are the ones that you are studying in this chapter. Although you have met them in the context of a computer passage, you may find some of them in other types of textbooks, newspapers, magazines, professional journals, and recreational reading sources as well.

1. **application** (ap li kā′ shən), *n.* **1.** a task that can be done by a computer. **2.** the act of applying. **3.** anything that is applied, like a cosmetic. **4.** a request or a form used to make a request, as a *job application.* **5.** capacity for use.

2. **cyberspace** (sī′ bər spās), *n.* the space of electronic movement of ideas and information.

3. **direct or dedicated link** (də rekt′ or de di kā tid link) a connection that provides complete, quick, and easy access to Internet functions.

4. **domain code** (dō mān′ kōd) the last part of an Internet address that identifies the geographical description or organizational identification.

5. **domain name** (dō mān′ nām) the part of an Internet address that refers to the particular organization.

6. **domain name system (DNS)** (dō mān′ nām sis′ təm) an addressing system used on the Internet to assign names and numbers to people and computers.

7. **e-mail** (ē māl) a way of sending an electronic message or letter between individuals or computers.

8. **Internet** (in′ tər net), *n.* a giant worldwide network that connects computer systems throughout the world that are willing to share their resources.

9. **Internet service providers** (in′ tər net sər′ vis prə vī′ dərs) national service providers that provide access to the Internet and other electronic services for a fee.

10. **modem** (mō′ dəm), *n.* an electronic device that enables microcomputers to communicate across telephone lines.

11. **netiquette** (net′ i ket), *n.* conventional requirements regarding proper social behavior when using the Internet.

12. **packets** (pak′ its), *n.* the units into which a message is broken down before it is sent over the Internet for reassembly with other packets when they reach their destination.

13. **provider or host computer** (prə vī′ dər or hōst kəm pyoo̅′ tər) organizations that offer access and a path for connection to the Internet.

14. **retrieval** (ri trē′ vəl), *n.* the act of finding or recovering stored information via a computer.

15. **SLIP (serial line internet protocol)** or **PPP (point to point protocol)**
(sēr′ ē əl līn in′ tər net prō′ tə kôl) a type of connection to the Internet using a modem and special software that connects the client to a provider.

16. **surf** (sûrf), *v.* a search technique used to find information on the Web or Internet. It typically involves navigating or exploring all the links you find to identify additional information on a subject.

17. **TCP/IP (transmission control protocol/internet protocol)**
(trans mish′ ən kən trōl′ prō′ tə kôl) rules for exchanging data between computers on the Internet.

18. **terminal connection** (tər′ min əl kə nek′ shən) a connection to the Internet using a modem and telephone lines that allows your computer to become part of a terminal network. It operates as a terminal that simply displays the communication that occurs between the computer and other computers on the Internet.

19. **user name** (yoo′ zər nām) the part of an Internet address that identifies a unique person or computer at the listed domain.

20. **virtual** (vûr′ chōō əl), *adj.* temporarily simulated or extended by computer software; as a *virtual community* created on the Internet or a *virtual shopping mall* on the Web.

Exercise 4: Matching

Match the terms in column A with their definitions in column B.

		Column A	*Column B*
_____	1.	packets	a. simulated by computer software
_____	2.	terminal connection	b. a search technique to find information on the Web
_____	3.	host computer or provider	c. the space of electronic movement or ideas
_____	4.	virtual	d. a worldwide network that connects computer systems
_____	5.	domain name system	e. the units into which an Internet message is broken down
_____	6.	cyberspace	f. an electronic device that enables computers to communicate across telephone lines
_____	7.	modem	g. an organization that offers access and a path for connection to the Internet.
_____	8.	surf	h. a connection between your computer and a terminal network on the Internet
_____	9.	domain code	i. an addressing system used on the Internet
_____	10.	Internet	j. the organizational identification part of an Internet address

	Column A	Column B

_____ 11. SLIP or PPP

k. the individual identification part of an Internet address

_____ 12. netiquette

l. a task that can be done by a computer

_____ 13. retrieval

m. a way of sending electronic messages or letters between individual computers

_____ 14. user name

n. the act of finding or recovering stored computer information

_____ 15. Internet service providers

o. a type of connection using a modem and special software that connects the client to a provider

_____ 16. application

p. the part of an Internet address that refers to the particular organization

_____ 17. direct link

q. rules of behavior for Internet communication

_____ 18. TCP/IP

r. national companies that provide access to the Internet and other electronic services for a fee

_____ 19. e-mail

s. a connection that provides direct, quick, and easy access to the Internet

_____ 20. domain name

t. rules for exchanging information between computers on the Internet

Exercise 5: Fill-In

Choose the word that best completes each sentence below and write its letter in the space provided.

a. modem	d. domain name	f. virtual	i. Internet service
b. surf	system	g. direct link	provider
c. user name	e. application	h. e-mail	j. retrieval

_____ 1. For two weeks after he got on the Internet, Jean-Claude's friends could not reach him since he spent all his free time

learning to _____ the Internet.

_____ 2. At the first class meeting, Professor Lynch gave her students her Internet address and told them they should

communicate with her via _____ .

_____ 3. The _____ of information or files that are not correctly named and saved can be difficult.

_____ 4. While planning her European vacation, Danisha logged onto

a home page called _____ Tourist that enabled her to simulate a visit to Paris.

_____ 5. In order to be able to connect her home computer with the ones in her office, Debbie purchased a high-speed

_____ and special software.

_____ 6. The technology director explained to the faculty and

professional staff that the _____ would identify their institution as a college by the letters *edu* at the end of everyone's e-mail address.

_____ 7. Although their company is new and small, Ray and Cynthia

decided that the cost of a _____ to the Internet would be money well spent.

_____ 8. Tameka's *Introduction to Your New Computer* course amazed

her with the introduction of a new _____ at every session.

_____ 9. As her _____ , the librarian chose *Konan,* and her patrons found it very easy to remember.

_____ 10. *America Online* is a very popular and active _____ with many subscribers around the country.

Exercise 6: Application

A friend of yours has just bought a new computer, and she is considering getting on-line. Briefly explain to her how the Internet works, how she can get access to the Internet, and what she will need to do to send and receive e-mail.

_____

_____

_____

_____

_____

ANSWERS TO EXERCISES

CHAPTER 1

Check your answers for the short-answer exercises in Chapter 1.

Exercise 3-Definitions

(Student answers will vary.) The definitions provided here are simpler than the dictionary-type definitions included in the word list.

1. paralanguage: the way we say something
2. modify: change, alter, adapt
3. competent: able, good at something
4. articulation: the way you express something in words
5. pitch: how high or low a voice or musical note is
6. perceived: interpreted, seen as
7. insecure: lacking confidence, shy
8. vocal fillers: sounds (uh, um) used to fill empty spaces in speech
9. excessively: too much
10. quality: characteristic feature
11. tempo: speed, pace
12. resonance: quality of speech affected by vibrations
13. rhythm: pattern of speech
14. kinesics: body movements or body language
15. emblems: body movements that stand for something; symbolic gestures
16. inappropriate: out of line, unacceptable behavior
17. illustrators: gestures used to demonstrate or help others visualize
18. regulators: signals or gestures that control a conversation
19. displays of feelings: showing how you feel through facial expressions or gestures
20. jutting: sticking out

Exercise 4: Matching

1. j	11. m		
2. i	12. t		
3. e	13. n		
4. f	14. o		
5. a	15. s		
6. h	16. r		
7. c	17. p		
8. d	18. k		
9. g	19. l		
10. b	20. q		

Exercise 5: Fill-In

1. b	
2. f	
3. a	
4. g	
5. h	
6. e	
7. c	
8. j	
9. d	
10. i	

CHAPTER 2

Check your answers for the short-answer exercises in Chapter 2.

Exercise 3-Definitions

(Student answers will vary.) The definitions provided here are simpler than the dictionary-type definitions included in the word list.

1. profession: career
2. evolving: changing
3. complexity: the quality of having parts or complications; intricacy
4. criterion: standard
5. practitioners: people who engage in a profession or activity
6. dilemmas: problem situations
7. vital: necessary, essential
8. allocation: distribution
9. auditing: examining the books
10. management
   advisory services: providing advice about running a business
11. mergers: the joining or combinations of two companies
12. enterprise: business venture or undertaking
13. controller: chief financial officer
14. transactions: business or financial activities
15. discloses: reveals, tells
16. entity: something that exists, like a business

17. data: information
18. deficient: lacking or missing something; substandard
19. compliance: in agreement; going along with; obeying
20. pursue: follow (a path or a person)

Exercise 4-Matching

1. d	11. o
2. h	12. p
3. g	13. n
4. f	14. q
5. b	15. s
6. i	16. k
7. j	17. t
8. a	18. m
9. c	19. l
10. e	20. r

Exercise 5-Fill-in

1. g
2. e
3. c
4. h
5. b
6. j
7. a
8. d
9. f
10. i

CHAPTER 3

Check your answers for the short-answer exercises in Chapter 3.

Exercise 3-Definitions

(Student answers will vary.) The definitions provided here are simpler than the dictionary-type definitions included in the word list.

1. life span: how long someone lives
2. embryological
   development: growth that occurs between conception and birth
3. fertilization: impregnation; the joining of an egg and sperm
4. proliferate: grow, spread
5. profound: significant, important
6. maturation: growth, development
7. puberty: the stage at which reproduction becomes possible
8. adulthood: the life stage where growth stops
9. ceases: stops, ends
10. sustained: continued
11. immune: resistant; biologically defensive

12. capacities: abilities
13. conception: the point at which fertilization takes place and an embryo begins
14. altering: changing; modifying
15. progressive: gradually changing
16. cumulative: growing by additions
17. incapacity: lacking in ability
18. senescence: old age accompanied by the loss of some bodily capacities
19. monitor: check on; watch or observe
20. chronological: time order

Exercise 4-Matching

1. e		11. p	
2. h		12. n	
3. f		13. r	
4. g		14. k	
5. b		15. t	
6. d		16. s	
7. i		17. m	
8. j		18. l	
9. c		19. o	
10. a		20. q	

Exercise 5-Fill-in

1. d
2. b
3. c
4. j
5. a
6. e
7. h
8. g
9. f
10. i

CHAPTER 4

Check your answers for the short-answer exercises in Chapter 4.

Exercise 3-Definitions

(Student answers will vary.) The definitions provided here are simpler than the dictionary-type definitions included in the word list.

1. family: any group of people united by marriage, ancestry, or adoption, usually involved in raising children
2. ancestry: one's family lineage or descent; your family history
3. collective: together, as a group
4. resources: what is available
5. incest taboo: the practice of forbidding sex between blood relatives
6. socialize: teach someone the ways of society and acceptable behavior

7. raw recruits: new members who don't know the routine yet

8. disabled: handicapped in some way

9. intricate web: complicated arrangement or system

10. ascribed statuses: social positions assigned because of who we are (e.g. a black female or a male teenager) rather than what we have achieved

11. ethnic: relating to someone's racial, national, or religious group

12. paternity: fatherhood

13. kin: blood relatives

14. monogamy: marriage to one person at a time

15. polygamy: marriage to more than one person at a time

16. polygyny: polygamy when a man has more than one wife

17. polyandry: polygamy when a woman has more than one husband

18. nuclear family: a basic social unit consisting of a husband, wife, and children

19. family of orientation: the family you are born into consisting of parents and children

20. family of procreation: the family you start by marrying and having children

Exercise 4-Matching

1. e
2. i
3. c
4. a
5. j
6. h
7. d
8. b
9. g
10. f
11. n
12. q
13. o
14. t
15. p
16. m
17. r
18. k
19. l
20. s

Exercise 5-Fill-in

1. c
2. g
3. f
4. a
5. d
6. i
7. b
8. e
9. g
10. j

CHAPTER 5

Check your answers for the short-answer exercises in Chapter 5.

Exercise 3-Definitions

(Student answers will vary.) The definitions provided here are simpler than the dictionary-type definitions included in the word list.

1. disregard: ignore; disrespect
2. essentially: by its nature
3. dispose (of):   get rid of; sell
4. consent: agree, go along with
5. violation: wrong, crime; an act that goes against what is right
6. barred: kept from; excluded; not allowed in
7. aligned: lined up; in agreement with
8. abolitionist: someone against slavery
9. abridged: shortened; limited
10. amendment: change; formal addition to a law or document
11. ratification: approval; consent; vote to accept
12. forefront: in the front line; pioneer position
13. initiatives: new moves; changes
14. prohibits: forbids; prevents
15. discrimination: unfair treatment based on the group you belong to
16. incumbent: someone already in office, e.g. a person who is running for re-election
17. gubernatorial: related to the office of governor, e.g. gubernatorial election
18. potent: strong, powerful
19. virtually: just about all; almost (synonym for essentially)
20. partisan: in favor of one group, as in Republican or Democratic

Exercise 4-Matching

1. d	11. p
2. j	12. t
3. f	13. o
4. g	14. q
5. h	15. k
6. b	16. n
7. i	17. r
8. c	18. l
9. a	19. s
10. e	20. m

Exercise 5-Fill-in

1. d
2. b
3. g
4. h
5. j
6. e
7. i
8. f
9. c
10. a

CHAPTER 6

Check your answers for the short-answer exercises in Chapter 6.

Exercise 3-Definitions

(Student answers will vary.) The definitions provided here are simpler than the dictionary-type definitions included in the word list.

1. controversy: hot issue; subject causing people to have strong opinions
2. explicit: clear; graphic; leaving nothing hidden
3. solo: alone, often performing
4. sadomasochism: sex involving pain
5. homoeroticism: sexually explicit or graphic homosexuality
6. saga: a long story
7. denounced: put down; criticized; ridiculed
8. obscene: offensive; usually involving sexual matter or vulgar language
9. furor: uproar; hysteria; often an overreaction to something
10. acclaim: praise, applause
11. itinerary: planned route for a trip
12. pornography: material designed for sexual arousal without any other purpose
13. duration: how long something lasts
14. censorship: someone else deciding what is acceptable in writing, art, etc.
15. exerted: pushed; put forward
16. totalitarian: government that allows little freedom
17. pluralistic: having different groups
18. rigidly: strictly; without flexibility
19. facilitating: easing; helping; assisting
20. resolution: ending; solution; settlement

Exercise 4-Matching

1. d	11. o
2. g	12. s
3. a	13. l
4. i	14. r
5. h	15. k
6. j	16. m
7. f	17. t

Exercise 5-Fill-in

1. b
2. g
3. f
4. c
5. j
6. e
7. a

8. c	18. q		8. h
9. e	19. p		9. i
10. b	20. n		10. d

CHAPTER 7

Check your answers for the short-answer exercises in Chapter 7.

Exercise 3-Definitions

(Student answers will vary.) The definitions provided here are simpler than the dictionary-type definitions included in the word list.

1. instrument: a device for making musical sounds
2. string: an instrument with a stretched string as the sound generator (guitar)
3. woodwind: an instrument with a column of air as the sound generator (flute)
4. brass: a metal instrument with a cup-shaped mouthpiece that uses a column of air as the sound generator (trombone)
5. percussion: an instrument that generates sound from its own material by striking, beating, or ringing (cymbals)
6. keyboard: an instrument with a pianolike set of keys
7. electronic: an instrument that uses electricity to generate or amplify sound
8. register: the range of a voice or instrument
9. flexible: adaptable; changeable
10. octaves: a series of eight notes in sequence in a range
11. dynamics: variation in volume
12. tones: sounds with a definite pitch
13. rites: formal or religious ceremonies or celebrations
14. enacted: acted out; portrayed
15. bolster: boost; support
16. aspired: wished; aimed for; strove toward
17. currency: timeliness; popularity at a particular time
18. implications: what is suggested or hinted as a result of something
19. resurrection: bringing something back to life; restoration
20. replicas: copies; reproductions

Exercise 4-Matching

1. d	11. t
2. i	12. r

Exercise 5-Fill-in

1. c
2. b

3. g	13. n	3. h	
4. h	14. q	4. g	
5. a	15. k	5. i	
6. j	16. l	6. a	
7. c	17. p	7. d	
8. e	18. s	8. e	
9. f	19. o	9. f	
10. b	20. m	10. j	

CHAPTER 8

Check your answers for the short-answer exercises in Chapter 8.

Exercise 3-Definitions

(Student answers will vary.) The definitions provided here are simpler than the dictionary-type definitions included in the word list.

1. rudimentary: basic, fundamental

2. physiologist: one who studies the body and its functions

3. secretion: a substance given off or produced, usually by a gland in the body

4. salivation: the production of saliva, a watery fluid, in the mouth

5. classical   the process of pairing one stimulus with another so the previously neutral
   conditioning: stimulus produces the same response the other one did naturally

6. neutral stimulus: a stimulus that produces no particularly distinct response on its own

7. unconditioned
   stimulus: a stimulus that brings about an automatic, natural response

8. elicits: brings out, draws forth, produces

9. unconditioned
   response: a response that occurs naturally without training

10. conditioned   a once-neutral stimulus that now produces a response because it has been
    stimulus: paired with another stimulus

11. conditioned
    response: a response that is produced by a conditioned stimulus

12. sequence: order

13. precedes: comes before

14. initial: first, beginning

15. pangs: pains, feelings of distress

16. evoked: brought about, produced, called forth

17. condemned: publicly and strongly criticized

18. ethically: morally, with integrity or going along with what is right
19. subtly: in an understated manner, delicately
20. prior: before

Exercise 4-Matching

1. d	11. q
2. f	12. o
3. h	13. l
4. g	14. m
5. b	15. r
6. c	16. t
7. e	17. n
8. i	18. s
9. j	19. k
10. a	20. p

Exercise 5-Fill-in

1. b
2. g
3. e
4. a
5. f
6. c
7. j
8. d
9. h
10. i

CHAPTER 9

Check your answers for the short-answer exercises in Chapter 9.

Exercise 3-Definitions

(Student answers will vary.) The definitions provided here are simpler than the dictionary-type definitions included in the word list.

1. equation: an algebraic expression in which the quantities on either side of the equal sign are equal
2. variable: a symbol used to represent an unspecified quantity
3. unspecified: not stated or unknown
4. elements: parts; members of a set
5. replacement set: the group of elements or numbers from which the value of the variable (x) can be chosen
6. constant: a symbol whose value does not change, e.g. 8
7. symbol: something that stands for something else
8. algebraic expression: a meaningful form consisting of numbers and letters with signs to indicate math operations
9. mathematical operations: procedures like addition or subtraction indicated by signs
10. entity: a quantity or thing that has an independent existence

11. term: two or more algebraic expressions treated as one and joined by plus or minus signs

12. factor: two or more algebraic expressions joined by multiplication

13. identify: make known; point out; figure out

14. evaluate: figure out the value or worth of something

15. calculate: do mathematical operations

16. concisely: briefly; without excess words or explanations

17. compact: dense; packed close together; a smaller version

18. translate: put into another language, other words, or symbols

19. solve: figure out the answer or the solution to a problem

20. applied: put to a useful purpose

Exercise 4-Matching

1. i   11. p
2. g   12. s
3. b   13. t
4. h   14. l
5. f   15. k
6. j   16. r
7. c   17. n
8. d   18. o
9. e   19. m
10. a   20. q

Exercise 5-Fill-in

1. d
2. g
3. b
4. e
5. a
6. h
7. f
8. j
9. i
10. c

CHAPTER 10

Check your answers for the short-answer exercises in Chapter 10.

Exercise 3-Definitions

(Student answers will vary.) The definitions provided here are simpler than the dictionary-type definitions included in the word list.

1. monument: an important person; a statue
2. save: except, but (no other definitions of the word work in the context)
3. cupolas: roof decorations
4. spires: the top part or point of something, like a steeple
5. encroached: pushed their way in

6. obliterated: covered up; pushed aside

7. august: respected; high and mighty

8. coquettish: "cutesie" (This one is very hard to get from the context and will require explanation. Just as a coquettish woman tries to appear attractive, the house was still trying to appear attractive although it was old and run-down.)

9. eyesore: a dump

10. bemused: confused (This is a tough one, too. Perhaps the cedar trees did not really belong in the cemetery.)

11. edict: rule or law

12. remitted: excused from paying (Although it works in context and is another definition of the word, paid is not an acceptable answer. Colonel Sartoris did not pay Miss Emily's taxes. He just said she didn't have to pay them.)

13. dispensation: pardon, excuse, or freedom from obligation

14. perpetuity: forever

15. archaic: old-fashioned

16. calligraphy: fancy writing

17. deputation: designated group

18. motes: bits, specks, or particles

19. gilt: gold (This one can't be figured out from context. As an example, paintings in museums often have gilt frames.)

20. hue: color or shade

Exercise 4-Matching

1. d	11. n
2. g	12. p
3. e	13. q
4. h	14. r
5. i	15. m
6. a	16. t
7. b	17. s
8. j	18. l
9. c	19. o
10. f	20. k

Exercise 5-Fill-in

1. a
2. d
3. j
4. h
5. b
6. f
7. i
8. c
9. g
10. e

CHAPTER 11

Check your answers for the short-answer exercises in Chapter 11.

Exercise 3-Definitions

(Student answers will vary.) The definitions provided here are simpler than the dictionary-type definitions included in the word list.

1. Internet: a worldwide network of computers that share information

2. cyberspace: the space of electronic exchange of information

3. virtual: not real but seemingly real; simulated

4. applications: specific things that computers can do

5. surf: to browse or move around on the Internet

6. provider or host computer: computer that is connected directly to the Internet and provides access for other computers

7. Internet service providers: companies that provide access to the Internet for a fee, like *America Online*

8. direct or dedicated link: a direct connection to the Internet; expensive and fast

9. retrieval: finding or recovering information that is stored on a computer

10. modem: an electronic device that lets computers talk to each other over telephone lines

11. SLIP or PPP: a type of connection to the Internet using a modem and special software

12. terminal connection: a type of connection that lets your computer become part of a terminal network, but its operations are limited

13. packets: the small units into which electronic messages are broken down before they are sent

14. TCP/IP: the protocols or rules that govern how and when computers talk to one another on the Internet

15. e-mail: a way to send electronic messages or letters to computers or individuals on the Internet

16. domain name system: an address system that is used to communicate on the Internet

17. domain code: the last part of the address that identifies the type of organization, like *edu* or *org*.

18. domain name: the part of the address that refers to the particular organization, like *mccc* refers to Mercer County Community College

19. user name: the part of the address that identifies the individual person or computer

20. netiquette: the rules of acceptable behavior for communicating on the Internet

Exercise 4-Matching

1. e	11. o
2. h	12. q
3. g	13. n
4. a	14. k
5. i	15. r
6. c	16. l
7. f	17. s
8. b	18. t
9. j	19. m
10. d	20. p

Exercise 5-Fill-in

1. b
2. h
3. j
4. f
5. a
6. d
7. g
8. e
9. c
10. i

BIBLIOGRAPHY

Barnett, Raymond and Kearns, Thomas J. From *Algebra for College Students* by Raymond A. Barnett and Thomas J. Kearns. Copyright © 1995 by The McGraw-Hill Companies. Reprinted with permission of The McGraw-Hill Companies.

Benjamin, Clinton L., et al. From *Human Biology* by Clinton L. Benjamin, Gregory R. Garman and James H. Funston. Copyright © 1997 by The McGraw-Hill Companies. Reprinted with permission of The McGraw-Hill Companies.

Calhoun, Craig et al. From *Sociology*, *7e* by Craig Calhoun, Donald Light and Suzanne Keller. Copyright © 1997 by The McGraw-Hill Companies. Reprinted with permission of The McGraw-Hill Companies.

Faulkner, William. "A Rose for Emily" from *Collected Stories of William Faulkner* by William Faulkner. Copyright © 1930 renewed 1958 by William Faulkner. Reprinted by permission of Random House, Inc.

Feldman, Robert S. From *Understanding Psychology*, *4e* by Robert S. Feldman. Copyright © 1996 by The McGraw-Hill Companies. Reprinted with permission of The McGraw-Hill Companies.

Gilbert, Rita. From *Living with Art* by Rita Gilbert. Copyright © 1995 by The McGraw-Hill Companies. Reprinted with permission of The McGraw-Hill Companies.

Hybels, Saundra and Weaver, Richard. From *Communicate Effectively*, *4e*. Copyright © 1995 by The McGraw-Hill Companies. Reprinted by permission of The McGraw-Hill Companies.

Kamien, Roger. From *Music: An Appreciation*, *6e* by Roger Kamien. Copyright © 1996 by The McGraw-Hill Companies. Reprinted with permission of The McGraw-Hill Companies.

Meigs, Robert et al. From *Accounting: The Basis for Business Decisions,10e* by Robert F. Meigs, Mary A. Meigs, Mark Bettner and Ray Whittington. Copyright © 1996 by The McGraw-Hill Companies. Reprinted with permission of The McGraw-Hill Companies.

O'Leary, Timothy J. and O'Leary, Linda. From *Computing Essentials 1997-1998 Multimedia Edition* by Timothy J. O'Leary and Linda O'Leary. Copyright © 1997 by The McGraw-Hill Companies. Reprinted with permission of The McGraw-Hill Companies.

Patterson, Thomas E. From *The American Democracy*, *3rd* edition by Thomas E. Patterson. Copyright © 1996 by The McGraw-Hill Companies. Reprinted with permission of The McGraw-Hill Companies.

Dictionaries consulted in creating this text include the following:

Merriam-Webster, Inc. *The Merriam Webster Dictionary,* Springfield, Mass.: Merriam-Webster, Inc., 1994.

Random House *Webster's College Dictionary.* New York: Random House, 1991.

Davies, Peter, ed. *The American Heritage Dictionary of the English Language.* Paperback edition. New York: Dell Publishing Co., 1980.

Funk & Wagnalls. *Funk & Wagnalls Standard Dictionary.* New York: Harper-Collins, 1980.